Revise

Mark's Gospel for GCSE

Simon and Christopher Danes

LION EDUCATIONAL
Oxford · Batavia · Sydney

For Roger, Jill, Sarah and Stephen

Copyright © 1993 Simon and Christopher Danes

The authors assert the moral right
to be identified as the authors of this work

Published by
Lion Publishing plc
Sandy Lane West, Oxford, England
ISBN 0 7459 2506 5

Albatross Books Pty Ltd
PO Box 320, Sutherland, NSW 2232, Australia
ISBN 0 7324 0672 2

First edition 1993

Acknowledgments
Bible text is reproduced from the Good News Bible
© American Bible Society, New York, 1966, 1971 and 4th edition 1976,
 published by the Bible Societies/HarperCollins

A catalogue record for this book is available
from the British Library

Printed and bound in Great Britain
by Blackmore Press, Shaftesbury

Contents

PART **1**

How to revise

Anyone who wanted to make a fortune should invent a machine for GCSE candidates which would revise for them. Unfortunately, there is no such thing. If you want to succeed, it is up to you.

Success depends on hard work

One of the most painless ways to revise is to review your work throughout the course. If you look back through your notes and texts during the holidays, for any subject, it will help to keep it fresh in your memory. If you are using this book while you are still doing your course, frequently reviewing your work will help you when it comes to the final exam. If you are preparing to sit the GCSE itself, it does not matter if you have not been doing this. However, you will need to work harder than the person who has.

For the paper on Mark's Gospel, the single most important thing to know is the text of the Gospel itself. You should know it **inside out**. The memory test section in this guide will help you test your knowledge. Of course, you will also need to know what it means, both when it was written and today. You will need to have the skills to do the evaluation questions. Your own notes, which you should have made during the course, will be important here. The *Revision notes* section in this guide will also help.

How much work do you need to do? Unless you are a genius with a photographic memory, the answer is clear—a lot. This is especially true if you are aiming for a high grade. (Presumably you are, or you would not have bought this book!) The worked example below gives you some idea of how much time you should set aside.

A very efficient way to revise is simply by reading: reading your notes, reading Mark's Gospel itself, reading your textbook, reading *Revision notes* in this book. However, if you read a piece of material once only, it is unlikely to stick. Three times is much better—perhaps even more.

Suppose you decide to read Mark's Gospel three times. The Gospel is about thirty pages long. If you read about thirty pages in an hour, to read the Gospel three times, you will need **3 hours**. (It would be a good idea to read it through each time on different days!)

Suppose you have also made 160 pages of notes on Mark during the course. Since your handwriting will probably be larger than the print used for Mark's text, assume you can read forty pages in an hour. To read your notes carefully through three times, you will need about **12 hours**.

If you decide to do some practice exam questions as well (there are some exam-type questions in this guide), you may need to add, say, another **1 hour**.

The total now comes to **16 hours**, and that is only for the paper on Mark!

Clearly, then, a good deal of work is needed if you want to do well. You will need to start revising well before the exams begin. Work out about how many hours in total you will need for all your revision. Be realistic! Draw up a revision timetable.

You will need to find the system of revising that suits you best. (The system that does not work is the system that requires little or no effort!) The lists of Dos and Don'ts below should give you some further help. Many of them apply not just to your revision for this RS paper, but to your revision for your other subjects as well.

Don'ts

● **Don't panic!**

● **Don't try silly methods of revising.**
Dictating all your notes onto a tape recorder will take ages. By the time you have finished, the exam will be over. And when will you have time to listen to them all?

   Writing out all your notes again is a waste of time. You might well find you are doing this mechanically, without concentrating. There is no point in it, anyway, because you already have a written copy of your notes! If you are still considering this method, think for a moment. How long does it take you to write a page? How long, then, will it take you to write ten pages? How long to write out all your notes again?

● **Don't waste time.**
It's very easy to do three minutes' work in an hour. You might spend the first five minutes arranging your pencils and pens on the desk, then look out of the window, then make a cup of coffee, then decide to telephone someone . . . Before you know it, the time you had earmarked for revision will have gone! Be strict with yourself and stick to your revision timetable.

● **Don't simply not bother working or rely on cramming it all in on one night before the exam. It doesn't work.**

● **Don't work in an atmosphere in which you cannot concentrate fully.**
Get away from the radio, CD or record player, television, dog, telephone or noisy younger brothers and sisters! If you cannot find somewhere to work in peace at home, try staying on after school or even going in before school starts. If that sounds too awful, try the public library.

● **Don't try to do anything else** which needs your concentration when you are revising. Music may be a good thing, but it will distract you. Do not believe those who claim otherwise! You need your full attention on your work if you are going to learn it most effectively. You cannot revise and watch the soaps at the same time, either.

● **Don't revise in bed.** You will fall asleep.

● **Don't stay in bed all day** when you are not in school. Getting up early gives you more time for work!

Dos

● **Do plan your day** as well as your revision timetable. If you are not in school, try to do three hours' work by lunchtime. This will break the back of it. If you are on study leave, try to do a full day's work (seven hours?). Getting into this routine will not only help you now, but will also help you if you are going on to an 'A' Level or other sixth form course. Revision in the sixth form is even more intensive than it is for GCSE. Start those good habits now!

● **Do use anything you find helpful**: spider diagrams, cue cards, highlighted notes, reduced notes . . . The brain remembers colours, so why not have multi-coloured or colour-coded notes? The method does not matter, as long as you remember the material.

● **Do read.**
If you decide to revise simply by reading your notes through, how many times do you need to do so? Are you going to read all your notes through once, then go back to the beginning and start again? Or are you going to read each section the set number of times before you go on to the next one?

- **Do plan your TV viewing and socializing.**
  Cut down the amount of television you watch. Is a limit of half an hour's viewing a day really going to hurt? Plan your socializing so that it does not interfere with your revision. There are lots of hours between getting home from school and going to bed. Can you find extra time in the early morning? Before school? At lunchtime? On the bus or train?

- **Do re-read the text of Mark's Gospel**, even if you are sure you know it. You cannot read it too many times. If you do not know the text properly, you will lose a lot of marks.

- **Do remember to look back at the text itself** when you revise your notes on Mark. If you are looking at the meaning of a parable, read the parable itself.

- **Do work hard!**

How to sit the exam

● **Don't panic!**

● **Do use your time properly.**
Take a watch in with you. Work out how much time you can allow for each question and try to stick to that. (In other words, do not spend three-quarters of your time on question one!)

● **Do read the paper through thoroughly before you start.**

● **Do check the rubrics** (the instructions on the front of the paper telling you how many questions to answer, and so on). Allow yourself a total of five minutes for all this. It is time well spent. This point cannot be overstated! **Every year, some candidates answer too many or too few questions.** The simple reason for this is that they have not read the rubric. They lose a large number of marks as a result. Don't let this happen to you: answer the correct number of questions.

Reading the paper through first is also important. As long as you follow the rubric, you can select the questions you think you can answer best.

If the very first thing you do in the exam room is to start to answer question one, you are not on line for a good grade.

● **Do check the number of marks available** for each question.
This will give you a good idea of how much you are expected to write. It is a waste of time writing a long paragraph for a one-mark question! Similarly, you cannot hope to get full marks on a four-mark question if you have only written a sentence.

(Remember that you are being marked on the quality of your answer. Four marks **does not** automatically mean that you must make four points. It **does** mean, though, that you will have to give a full and careful answer to gain all four marks.)

● **Do write as clearly as you can in good English.**
Usually, 5 per cent of your total marks assess the standard of your written English. So, write in your best English, use punctuation correctly, and spell as carefully as you can. It is astonishing how many candidates do not start sentences with capital letters or end them with full stops, or misspell words that are printed on the question paper.

● **Do answer the question!**
It seems daft to say this, but, once again, candidates often do not follow this simple advice. They may have misread the question. They may not have answered every part of the question. (It is common for people to answer the first part and then to overlook the second part. This costs them marks.) Remember: even a good answer to a non-existent question will not get you good marks!

● **Do answer in detail**.
A one-mark question will not need a detailed answer. However, make sure you go into as much detail as you can on your other answers. If you can make two points about a question, write down both of them. If you can give four reasons for your viewpoint, give all four of them. Explain your answer in as much detail as you can (always keeping your eye on the clock, of course).

Be careful: saying the same thing three times in different ways is not the same as making three different points! Repeating yourself will not get you extra marks.

Be careful, also, not to get a bee in your bonnet. Some candidates get a good idea, and then use it in every answer.

● **Do make sure your answer is relevant.**
It must answer the question and do no more than that. Be careful not to waffle. Some candidates want to write down everything they have learnt, regardless of whether or not it answers the question. If it does not answer the question, it will not help you.

● **Do try to allow yourself time to check your answers.**
  ▷ Are your answers correct?
  ▷ Have you answered in as much detail as you can? Or have you left something out that needs to be added?
  ▷ Have you answered the question set? Check with the question paper.
  ▷ Is your answer relevant? If it waffles, cut out the waffle!
  ▷ Have you numbered your answer correctly?

If you find you do not have time to check your answers, don't worry!

It is very important, however, to use all the time in every examination. So, if you do finish before the exam is over, check your answers. If you still have some time left, check them again. If there is *still* time left, check them again, and so on. Despite what other candidates may appear to think, exams are not a race. And dozing or staring into space are not particularly good ways to use time!

Be careful not to panic when you check your answers. Some candidates think that one of their answers is bound to be wrong. So they cross out the right answer and write in the wrong one! Keep a cool head, and think!

Don't be tempted to fill up any 'spare' time by answering an extra question. It will not get you any extra marks. It will also waste the time you could better use in checking your work.

Revision notes

Mark is one of the four Gospels. 'Gospel' translates the Greek word which means 'good news'.

Why were the Gospels written?

Four main reasons for writing the Gospels were:

1. **Jesus' disciples, the original witnesses, were dying off.** A permanent record was needed.

2. **Gentiles (non-Jews) came into the community of the Church.** They came in great numbers, from different religious backgrounds. There was a danger they might bring wrong ideas into Christianity. The Gospel writers wanted to put the record straight about Jesus.

3. **The Roman authorities needed to be shown that Christianity was not politically dangerous.**

4. **Christians needed to be encouraged in their faith.**

Who was Mark?

He may well have been the 'John Mark' who appears in Acts and in the letters of Paul and Peter. John Mark's home was in Jerusalem, and he was a travelling companion of Paul.

Christian tradition also links Mark with Peter, the leader of the disciples—Papias, writing 100 years after Jesus' crucifixion, makes this claim. He said this information came from a still earlier writer, who said that Mark was Peter's helper, and that he wrote down the stories Peter told when he was preaching.

We need to be slightly careful here. 'Mark' was a very common name in the Roman Empire. But if Mark was not John Mark, we know nothing about him.

When and where was Mark written?

The answer is, probably in AD 64–65 in Rome.

This would fit in with the fact that the Emperor Nero was killing Christians in Rome in AD 64. Paul and Peter died in this persecution. Mark emphasizes that his readers should stand firm in the face of trouble. This would fit with the Roman situation. He uses some Latin words instead of Greek ones. (The Gospel itself was written in Greek.)

Again, we cannot be certain. Some scholars believe there is not enough evidence. Others suggest the Gospel is even earlier. Few believe it to be later.

What were Mark's sources?

It is difficult to be certain about written sources, since we do not have them, if they ever existed. Mark would certainly have used stories about Jesus that circulated by word of mouth (orally). He may have consulted Peter.

Written sources may have been used for:

1. **The Passion** (the story of Jesus' suffering and death).

2. **The Little Apocalypse** (chapter 13, speaking of the end of the world).

3. **Some stories in Aramaic**, the language spoken in Palestine at that time. Peter and Jesus would have spoken Aramaic.

This section examines the following passages:

The preaching of John the Baptist	**1 : 1–8**
The death of John the Baptist	**6 : 14–29**

The preaching of John the Baptist
READ MARK 1 : 1–8

Mark opens his book by calling it the 'good news' or 'gospel'. The good news is about Jesus, who is the Messiah (Christ) and the Son of God. (See further on these titles in the *Stories about Jesus* section.)

John's coming fits in with the Old Testament: the prophets Isaiah and Malachi predicted that someone would arrive to prepare for the Messiah. The Jews believed this would be Elijah. John lived in the desert like Elijah, and his clothes—the camel-hair garment and the leather belt—are identical. Jesus later implies that John is the expected Elijah (Mark 9 : 13). John calls on the people to repent: to change their minds and their attitudes. He baptizes, or washes, them as a sign that they have done this. (Remember: this is not the same as Christian baptism, though Christian baptism grew out of it.)

The Messiah is so great, John says, that he is unworthy to undo the Messiah's sandal strap. This was a slave's duty for his master. The Messiah will baptize 'with the Holy Spirit'. This probably means he will bring people in touch with God in a new way. Mark's first readers might well be reminded here of their own baptisms.

Some scholars have suggested that John was once an Essene.

The **Essenes** lived a kind of monastic life. Some lived in towns; most lived in the Judean desert. They believed themselves to be the only true Jews, and they had strict rules. Many did not marry, or only did so to produce children. Training for the group was hard and long. They shared their property, and may have written the Dead Sea Scrolls, found at Qumran in 1948. Like John, they baptized their members—although unlike John, they baptized them more than once. They were also waiting for not one, but two (perhaps three) Messiahs.

The death of John the Baptist
READ MARK 6 : 14–29

The story starts with the theme, 'Who is Jesus?' People get the answer wrong: he is not John, he is not Elijah and he is not a prophet. He is greater than any of these.

The story of John's death, which is also told by the Jewish historian Josephus, is fairly straightforward. Herod Antipas ruled Galilee for the Romans. Strictly speaking, he was not a king, but a *tetrarch* (ruler). His family had a reputation for immorality. John spoke out against Herod and it cost him his life.

This section examines the following passages:

Jesus calls the first disciples	**1 : 14–20**
Jesus preaches in Galilee	**1 : 35–39**
Jesus calls Levi	**2 : 13–17**
Jesus calls the Twelve	**3 : 13–19**
Jesus sends out the Twelve	**6 : 7–13**

Jesus calls the first disciples
READ MARK 1 : 14–20

Jesus' words in verse 15 give Mark's summary of the whole of Jesus' message. It is deliberately placed at the beginning of Jesus' work. (See also the section *The Kingdom of God* later in the revision notes.)

'Disciples' means 'people who learn'. Other Jewish teachers had disciples. Jesus is unique in that he 'calls' his disciples. He does not wait for them to come to him, he seeks them out. Also, Jesus' disciples are ordinary people, not just educated men: his message is for all.

The four fishermen—Simon (Peter), Andrew, James and John—follow Jesus straight away. This is how Mark thinks people should respond to Jesus' call.

They will no longer catch fish: their catch will be people. They will get others to follow Jesus—to draw them into the 'net' of the Kingdom.

Jesus preaches in Galilee

READ MARK 1 : 35-39

Jesus and his disciples go on a preaching tour throughout Galilee.

Jesus prays early in the morning. He was a Jew and it was Jewish practice in his time, as it is now, to do this. But Mark may also want the people to understand what sort of a Messiah Jesus is: he needs strength to carry on his work, as he has just performed a large number of miracles.

Simon Peter and his 'companions' (probably the other disciples) find him. Everyone is looking for Jesus. Mark believed they still were, when he wrote, and Christians believe they still are today. People need Jesus, even if they do not realize it.

Jesus says they must go to the other villages, so that he can preach there, too, because 'that is why I came'. He has just come from Capernaum, but originally he came from God.

The preaching tour is dealt with in one verse, but it would have taken many months. 'Driving out demons' and 'preaching' are both the work of the Messiah, who brings in the Kingdom.

Jesus calls Levi

READ MARK 2 : 13-17

Levi may also have been called Matthew. He was a tax collector.

Tax collectors were hated because they worked for the Romans. They also took more than the government wanted, and kept the rest for themselves. Some became extremely rich. Their contact with Gentiles, and the fact that they often worked on the Sabbath, the Jewish holy day, made them ritually unclean—unfit to worship God.

Jesus' choice of Levi, then, is very shocking. Like the fishermen, Levi follows Jesus straight away. Mark shows that the Kingdom of God is for everybody, for outcasts like Levi, and those who eat with Jesus in the house as well.

The Pharisees, watching this, were extremely surprised.

The **Pharisees** were the largest religious party in Jesus' time. 'Pharisee' may mean 'someone who is separate from others'. They wanted to keep the Torah to the letter. The Torah is the Law of God, contained in the first five books of the Bible, believed to have been given by God to Moses. Some Pharisees had normal jobs; others studied the Torah full time. They wanted to ensure that they did not break the least of the Torah's rules, even by accident. So they made extra rules to make sure its laws were never broken.

For example, the Torah said people should not work on the Sabbath. This was probably to give people a day off, for rest and worship. The Pharisees tried to define what 'work' meant, to make sure the command was not broken. They said 'work' included walking more than two-thirds of a mile. Even writing was classified as 'work'. Such rules became very difficult to keep.

The Pharisees also believed in ideas found in other parts of the Jewish Bible, such as angels, life after death, and the coming of the Messiah.

The Pharisees would have been worried by Jesus' eating with people like Levi. Such people, they thought, were outcasts. Moreover, their food would not be 'kosher'—it would not be the right type of food, prepared in the way set down in the Torah.

Jesus replies to their objections by saying it is people who are ill who need a doctor, not people who are well. The outcasts are included in the Kingdom. Jews in Jesus' time sometimes pictured the Kingdom of God as a huge celebration meal: the Messiah's, or Messianic, Banquet. So, when Jesus eats with the tax collectors and sinners, it is a sign that they are being invited to the Messianic Banquet, the Kingdom of God.

Jesus calls the Twelve

READ MARK 3 : 13–19

The old Israel (the Jews) was divided into **twelve** tribes. The new people in the Kingdom have Jesus' **twelve** disciples at the centre.

They are also called 'apostles', which means 'people who are sent' or 'ambassadors'. They are to do three things:

1. **To be with Jesus** (as all Christians should be).

2. **To preach.** They are to spread the news about the Kingdom.

3. **To drive out demons.** This, again, is part of the work of the Messiah in bringing in the Kingdom. The disciples share in this work.

The disciples

▷ are shown to be ordinary people.

▷ are led by Peter (next to Jesus).

▷ would become the later Christian leaders. Some, including Peter and James, would die for their faith in Jesus.

▷ are not perfect. James and John are called 'Boanerges' or 'sons (men) of thunder', possibly because of their quick tempers. Peter denied that he knew who Jesus was.

▷ were believed to have written some of the books and letters in the New Testament (1 and 2 Peter, John's Gospel, Matthew's Gospel).

▷ included Judas. We cannot be sure why Jesus chose the man who would betray him.

▷ included at least one Zealot: the second Simon. (Judas and possibly James and John may also have been Zealots.)

The **Zealots** (meaning 'fanatics') believed in fighting against the Romans. They believed their king should not be Caesar, but God or someone whom God would appoint: the Messiah, who would lead them in battle. The Romans thought of the Zealots as terrorists. The fact that Jesus chose at least one Zealot as a disciple does not show he agreed with Zealots. It shows, again, that the Kingdom of God is for everybody.

Catholic Christians (Roman Catholic, Orthodox and most Anglicans) believe bishops to be the successors of the Twelve. Roman Catholics believe the Pope to be the successor of Peter.

Jesus sends out the Twelve

READ MARK 6 : 7–13

In their mission, the Twelve are to

▷ preach that people should repent—turn away from their sins;

▷ drive out demons;

▷ heal the sick.

All this shares in Jesus' work of bringing in the Kingdom of God. Mark thinks that the Church, following on from the disciples, also shares in this work of Jesus.

The disciples are to travel light. This shows they are to be completely dependent on God. They can take sandals and a stick, but no money, beggar's bowl, food or extra clothes. They must not stay anywhere too long or waste time on people who will not listen to them. They are not to beg, because wandering preachers in Jesus' time were sometimes dishonest. The disciples are not to be like that.

Jews returning from non-Jewish (Gentile) towns would shake the dust from their feet. The disciples must now do it for Jewish towns where people will not listen. Mark thinks times have changed. It no longer matters whether or not you are a Jew. What matters is whether or not you accept the apostles' teaching about the Kingdom. By shaking dust off their shoes, the apostles are warning people that they could be left outside the Kingdom.

The instructions to the disciples may also have been used by later Christian missionaries, perhaps in Mark's own time.

Section 3: Stories about Jesus

This section examines the following passages:

Jesus' baptism and temptation

READ MARK 1 : 9–13

Jesus first appears in Mark at the baptism.

Three things should be noticed:

1. **The heavens open.** Jewish writings which look forward to the Kingdom of God sometimes include the idea that God will open heaven (Isaiah 64 : 1, for example). The detail shows that the Kingdom is almost here.

2. **The Holy Spirit descends like a dove.** The Holy Spirit had inspired the Old Testament prophets. People thought he would return with the Messiah.

   The Spirit is said to descend 'like a dove', which may remind Mark's readers of the dove which brought the olive branch to Noah when the flood was over, or it may echo the story of creation in Genesis, when God's Spirit hovers (like a bird?) over the unmade world.

3. **There is a voice from heaven.** The voice of God uses words from Psalm 2 : 7, originally addressed to Israel's king, to say that Jesus is the Son of God.

   The voice also says God is pleased with Jesus. This echoes Isaiah 42 : 1, which tells of the Suffering Servant of God. The Suffering Servant died for the people. This is what Jesus will do.

Jesus, then, is called the **Son of God**. In the Old Testament, the king was called the son of God. The Messiah was the king (see below), so calling Jesus 'the Son of God' shows he is a kingly Messiah.

Jesus does not often call himself 'the Son of God', though he does not deny being the Son of God. He does not want people to get the wrong idea about the sort of Messiah he is. He is not the warrior king the Zealots hoped for: his path is one of suffering.

Christians soon came to realize that Jesus was God himself, made human. 'Son of God' became a good way of expressing this idea.

Mark does not go into details about Jesus' **temptation** by the Devil. 'Temptation' means 'being put to the test': as Jesus withstands the test of the Devil, he is ready to start his work. Mark may be telling his readers that they should not worry about being tempted to do wrong as long as they stand firm, perhaps in the face of persecution. After all, Jesus was tempted too.

The Jews believed the Kingdom of God would involve a struggle against the forces of evil. Jesus begins this battle against the Devil here, and it continues when he casts out demons.

Jesus is rejected at Nazareth

READ MARK 6 : 1–6

Jesus has been carrying on his mission for some time before he goes home. The people of Nazareth want to hear what he has to say for himself. So they go to the synagogue (the local place of worship). Yet they all know his family, and they cannot believe that their carpenter is anything special.

Jesus says that a prophet is welcome everywhere except at home, by his own people. This was a well-known proverb. They have no faith in Jesus or in the Kingdom. So Jesus can do nothing for them, except for a few healings. God can do nothing for people who do not want him.

Peter's declaration about Jesus

READ MARK 8 : 27—9 : 1

Before this point in the Gospels, the disciples have not said who they think Jesus is. Indeed, they have often been very confused. Some people have been saying Jesus is John the Baptist, Elijah, or another prophet.

Near Caesarea Philippi, Jesus asks them who they say he is. Peter replies that Jesus is the Christ (Messiah).

This is the right answer, but they must keep it to themselves. They and others must learn what the Messiah is to do: he is to suffer, die and to rise again.

Note: Jesus refers to himself here as the Son of Man, not such a loaded title as 'Messiah'. Nobody expected the Messiah to die a criminal's death, let alone rise again.

Peter certainly cannot take it in, so he tells Jesus off. Jesus angrily calls him 'Satan': the one who tempts people to do wrong.

Jesus then teaches the crowd what it means to follow him:

- They must be prepared to give up everything, and follow him to the death if necessary: to take up their cross.

- Those who do not want to do this, but prefer to cling to worldly things, will lose the most precious thing they have: themselves. People will find themselves fully in giving up everything for Jesus and for the gospel. Nothing can buy back a ruined and worthless life.

- Those who are ashamed of Jesus will find he is ashamed of them at his second coming.

- Some will not die before they see that the Kingdom of God has come. (This, 9 : 1, is a very difficult verse. It may mean that they will realize that the Kingdom is already here with Jesus. Or it may refer to the Transfiguration, which follows 9 : 1, or to the resurrection. Or it may show that some—*perhaps* including Jesus himself—thought the second coming would happen soon.) Jesus also predicts his suffering and death in 9 : 30–32 and 10 : 32–34. It is worth reading these verses. In the first passage, the disciples do not understand and are too afraid to ask. They remain very frightened in the second.

Peter calls Jesus 'the Christ' in this story. It is important to remember some information about this title:

▷ **Messiah** (Hebrew) and **Christ** (Greek) should both be translated as 'the anointed one'. In the Old Testament, kings were anointed. Therefore the Messiah was the king.

▷ The ancient kings of Israel were often less than ideal. In 587BC, the last king to be descended from the great King David was deposed by the Babylonians, and there were none after him. These two things made the Jews hope for an ideal king: *the* Messiah.

▷ In Jesus' time, many thought the Messiah would be a warrior who would throw the Romans out of Israel.

▷ The Essenes expected two (perhaps three) Messiahs. One would be a priest, the other a king.

▷ Jesus rejected his contemporaries' views. The Messiah's job was not to win a war, but to suffer, die and rise again.

The Transfiguration

READ MARK 9 : 2–13

The story of the Transfiguration shows Peter, James and John who Jesus really is. The account is like a code, which can be cracked:

- **It takes place on a mountain.**
  In the Old Testament, mountains symbolize places where people can be close to God.

- **Jesus is transfigured**, and his clothes become dazzling white.
  Heavenly things such as angels were pictured as being dressed in white. The human Jesus is shown also to be the Son of God.

- **The disciples are frightened.**
  In the Old Testament, people are often frightened when God does something.

- **Peter wants to make three shelters/tents/tabernacles.**
  The Jewish festival of Tabernacles recalled how the people lived in tents in the desert. Moses was their leader then. There was even a tent-shrine for God, who was particularly close to them. Peter thinks the time has come when God, in Jesus, will once again live with his people. But you cannot stick God's glory in a tent. God's glory is in Jesus, and in Jesus' work.

- **The cloud symbolizes God the Father's presence**, as it does in the Old Testament.

- **The voice repeats the words at the baptism**, and says that Jesus is the Son of God.
  People are to listen to Jesus. Jesus has just taught and will teach again that he must suffer.

- **Elijah, the greatest prophet, and Moses, the greatest law-giver, appear.**
  ▷ The Jews thought Elijah would arrive before the Messiah.
  ▷ Moses had predicted that God would send the people a new prophet.
  ▷ Elijah and Moses both suffered for their faith. Jesus will also suffer.
  ▷ The Law (Moses) and the prophets (Elijah) are fulfilled in Jesus.

After the Transfiguration, the disciples are again shown the other side of the coin. The Son of God must also suffer. Jesus implies, too, that Elijah did come before the Messiah arrived. Elijah's job was done by John the Baptist.

Section 4: The Kingdom of God

This section examines the following passages:

Jesus' mother and brothers	3 : 31–35
The parable of the sower and the purpose of the parables	4 : 1–20
More parables	4 : 21–34
Who is the greatest?	9 : 33–37
Some teaching of Jesus	9 : 38–50
Jesus blesses the children	10 : 13–16
The rich man	10 : 17–31
The widow's mite	12 : 41–44
James' and John's question	10 : 35–45

Most Jews in Jesus' time were looking forward to **God's rule**—the **Kingdom of God**. The Jews had been ruled by foreign powers for many centuries. In 587BC, the Babylonians conquered Judah, and their rule was followed by that of the Persians, then the Greeks, and finally the Romans.

The people began to hope for a time when God would be in charge. God would save them from their enemies, just as he had long ago saved them from the Egyptians when Moses was their leader. Instead of just another human kingdom, the Kingdom of God would arrive.

The Kingdom of God, then, meant that God would be in charge. But different Jews had different ideas of the way in which God would rule:

- the Zealots thought the Kingdom of God meant that the Jews would rule their own country. Jewish rule was God's rule, so a Jewish kingdom would also be the Kingdom of God. Once he had defeated the Romans, the Messiah would be their king.

● the Essenes thought it meant there would be a war against the powers of darkness. All evil powers and evil people would be destroyed. The paradise that followed would be the Kingdom of God.

Jesus' teaching shows he disagreed with both these views. He believed in the Kingdom of God, but thought that only God could bring it about. Just as only God can make a seed grow, only he can make the Kingdom come (Mark 4 : 26–29). The Kingdom would not involve a struggle against the Romans, but it *would* involve a struggle against

> ▷ sin, which Jesus forgives
> ▷ illness, which Jesus heals
> ▷ demons, whom Jesus defeats by exorcizing them (casting them out).

The Kingdom would also be a **new society**. It was not just about God ruling over the people, but also people living by God's laws. Also, the Kingdom was not just open to Jews. It was open to everybody. Sinners, outcasts and Gentiles could enter. The relationship with God in the Kingdom was not just for this life: after death, people would be happy with God for ever. The future with Jesus, which would continue after death, is the full and final arrival of the Kingdom.

Note: in some of Jesus' sayings about the Kingdom, he appears to expect it to arrive in the future. In others, he speaks as though it is already here. Scholars have different views about Jesus' teaching on the Kingdom:

1. Some think Jesus did not think the Kingdom had arrived, but that it would arrive in the future, perhaps in the near future.

2. Others think he never said it would arrive in the future: it was already here in its fullness.

3. Others think Jesus taught that the Kingdom had begun with his coming, but that it would arrive in its fullness later. This is the view of the Kingdom taken by Mark's Gospel.

Jesus' mother and brothers
READ MARK 3 : 31–35

The point of this story is that anyone who does what God wants is in the Kingdom. Those in the Kingdom are as close to Jesus as the members of his own family.

The parable of the sower and the purpose of the parables
READ MARK 4 : 1–20

Parables were stories used by teachers in Jesus' time. They got their point across by comparing one thing with another. Their imagery was usually drawn from people's everyday lives. Jesus' imagery often comes from farming.

Jesus' parables all teach about some aspect of the Kingdom of God.

The parable of the sower is unusual in that it is explained. Instead of the general picture being important, each part of the story represents something else. This type of parable is called an allegory. The parable is interpreted as follows:

The sower = the person spreading God's word (translated as 'message' in the Good News Bible).

The seed that fell on the path, eaten by the birds = those who hear the word, but have it taken away by Satan.

The seed on rocky ground, which grows quickly and dries up = those who receive the word gladly, but who have no staying power: when trouble or persecution comes, they give up.

The seed sown among thorns, which is choked = those who are too attached to the world, who do not accept the message properly.

The seed sown among good soil which produces corn = those who hear and accept the word and who 'bear fruit'.

Nearly all scholars believe that the interpretation of the parable of the sower is not part of Jesus' original teaching. It has been added later by the early Christians. This is partly because it has more to do with preaching the message of Christianity than with the coming of the Kingdom. Also, some of the vocabulary is more often found in early Christian writings than in Jesus' teaching (such as talk of persecution and calling the Christian message 'the word').

If this is right, then the original meaning of the parable seems to be that the Kingdom will come, despite its small beginnings. God is like a farmer who sows seed everywhere. (This is what happened when you sowed seed by hand.) Some finds good soil, other seed does not. Yet the harvest of the Kingdom will come. In verses 10–12, Jesus explains the purpose of the parables. For some people, they are riddles which are impossible to understand. People who have closed their minds remain outside the Kingdom: however hard they look, they will not understand anything. (Jesus borrows some language from the prophet Isaiah to get this point across.) The disciples, however, have been given the secret of the Kingdom. They may need to have some of the parables explained to them, but they are basically 'tuned in' to the Kingdom and will understand them.

It is possible that Mark thought Jesus deliberately wanted the parables to blind one group of people, who would remain outside the Kingdom. If so, Mark has missed the point. Parables were intended to make things easy to understand, not difficult.

More parables

READ MARK 4 : 21–34

This is probably Mark's own collection of parables. Jesus would not have preached all of them on one occasion.

A lamp under a bowl (4 : 21–23) shows that what is hidden will be brought into the open. Jesus' followers will see the Kingdom, and the truth about the Kingdom needs to be brought into the open and spread.

'The same rules you use to judge others will be used by God to judge you' (4 : 24) is hard to understand. Three possible explanations are:

1. God will judge people after death in the same way as they have judged others. (This idea influences the Good News Bible translation.)

2. Jesus is making the general comment that we get out of life what we put into it.

3. Jesus is again speaking of the Kingdom. If people are 'tuned in' to the Kingdom, their understanding will increase.

'The person who has something will be given more' (4 : 25) seems to mean that if you are already 'tuned in' to the parables, you will understand things even better. If your mind is closed, you will end up worse than you were in the first place. This could apply to the legalism of the Pharisees.

The growing seed (4 : 26–29) is the second parable of growth. The first was the parable of the sower.

Scholars used to think that these parables show that the Kingdom arrives gradually, just as a seed gradually turns into a plant. This rather misses the point. It is not important how long the process takes: the important thing is that the plant actually does appear. People will see that the Kingdom has come.

It is not clear who the farmer represents. If he represents God, God lets the world run on, and then brings in the harvest of the Kingdom. If, as seems more likely, the farmer represents Jesus' followers, their job is to sow the seed (the message) and then leave it to God to bring in the Kingdom. The Kingdom cannot be brought about by human actions, as the Zealots thought.

The mustard seed (4 : 30–32), another parable of growth, shows that the Kingdom will come as surely as a tiny seed grows into a huge plant. Jesus' work may seem to have little effect at the moment, but the Kingdom will arrive.

In the Old Testament 'birds' sometimes meant foreigners. The parable may be saying that foreigners (Gentiles) will be included in the Kingdom.

Why Jesus used parables. 4 : 33–34 shows that Jesus told other parables which Mark does not include. The reason Mark gives is similar to that in 4 : 10–12.

Who is the greatest?
READ MARK 9 : 33–37

The disciples' dispute about which of them is the greatest is resolved by Jesus' saying, 'Whoever wants to be first must place himself last of all and be the servant of all.' This is the way Jesus himself behaves.

Children are dependent and need to be looked after. If the disciples want to be great, they should help those who need to be looked after. If they welcome a child in Jesus' name, they are welcoming Jesus. If they welcome Jesus, they are welcoming God.

Being in the Kingdom is not about status or power. It is about serving others.

Some teachings of Jesus
READ MARK 9 : 38–50

'Whoever is not against us is for us.' 9 : 38–41 shows that the disciples should not be too possessive about their authority. They should not have told off the exorcist who did not belong to their group. After all, such outsiders could become followers of Jesus. The disciples should remember that anyone who does no more than give them a cup of water because they bear Christ's name will be rewarded.

Temptations to sin. 9 : 42–48 warns that some things people do will result in their being sent to hell. 'Hell' is the English word for *Gehenna*, which was a rubbish dump outside Jerusalem. The burning rubbish made it an effective symbol for the place where evil people would be punished after death.

Jesus is saying that if you cause someone—including yourself—to stumble, you will be punished. 'Stumble' may mean 'lose faith' (as the Good News Bible translates it). Or it may mean 'sin'.

It is a terrible fate to be drowned with a millstone around your neck. Yet it is even more terrible to cause 'one of these little ones' (either children *or* simply 'Christians') to stumble.

Jesus also warns his followers not to let themselves stumble. They should want the life of the Kingdom. It is far more important even than a hand, or a foot, or an eye.

Salt (verses 49–50). A hard passage. It may mean that Christians should be pure, or that they may have to suffer the fire of persecution. If Christians lose their purity, they will be no use to anyone.

Jesus blesses the children
READ MARK 10 : 13–16

The Kingdom of God belongs to people like children. Children can be seen as eager to learn, trusting and loving. This is the way Christians should be towards God. But children are of course not always like this, so the point seems to be wider. Children in Jesus' day had little social standing, so the Kingdom of God belongs to others like them: the poor, the oppressed and the outcasts.

Those who do not receive the Kingdom of God like a child will not enter it. Children generally do not turn their noses up at things done especially for them. The disciples should have this child-like openness towards the gift of the Kingdom.

The rich man
READ MARK 10 : 17–31

It was good that the rich man kept the rules of the Torah, but his money was stopping him getting closer to God. The Jewish view was that money was a gift from God. So the disciples were amazed: if it is going to be hard for the rich to enter the Kingdom, it is going to be even harder for the poor! But this misses the point. The coming of the Kingdom changes things. The Kingdom is the most important thing there is and nothing must get in the way—money, or even family and friends. People who give everything up for the Kingdom will be rewarded with new 'brothers', 'sisters' and 'mothers' among their fellow-Christians in the Church, and also with eternal life. People cannot enter the Kingdom by their own efforts. It is easier to push a camel through the eye of a needle than to squeeze a rich person into God's Kingdom. But then nothing is impossible for God.

In the Kingdom, the tables will be turned. Many of the first will be last, and many of the last will be first. Those whom the world thinks are the most important will be the last to squeeze into the Kingdom, and will not be the most important in it. But those whom the world thinks are the least important will be the first into the Kingdom, and perhaps the most important people in it as well.

(The correct attitude to wealth is shown in the story of the widow's mite—see Mark 12 : 41–44.)

Jesus said to the rich man, 'sell all you have and give the money to the poor.' This certainly shows that Christians should care for the poor. But did Jesus mean that everybody should give away all their possessions? Is it bad to be rich?

Here are some possible answers:

▷ Jesus was talking to one man. He did not mean everybody.
▷ Money is only bad if you make it into an idol. However, if you have money you should use it to help others.
▷ Only some people have the strength to do what Jesus told the rich man to do. That is why monks and nuns take a vow of poverty and live without possessions.
▷ Christians should share their possessions, as did the earliest Christians in the Acts of the Apostles. Christians simply fail to live up to the standards Jesus set.

James' and John's question

READ MARK 10 : 35–45

James and John want positions of power in Jesus' Kingdom. Again, they have missed the point. The Kingdom is not about power but about service.

If the Messiah's job is to suffer and die to redeem many, then his disciples should be ready to suffer for others. They should be ready to share the cup and the baptism of Jesus' suffering.

James and John did remain faithful to Jesus. James was executed for his faith, though we do not know whether or not this happened to John.

Mark's readers would have been reminded here of the cup used at the Eucharist, and of their own baptism. Both are linked to suffering. Mark may well be reminding his readers, who may have been persecuted by Nero, what their faith means.

Jesus cannot grant favours to his friends: the Father has already decided who is to have the chief places in the Kingdom. They will certainly not go to bigheads who want power. The most important people in the Kingdom are those who do most to help others: 'Even the Son of Man did not come to be served; he came to serve and to give his life to redeem many people.'

(For the allegory of the vineyard, see the section on *Controversy Stories*.)

Section 5: Miracles

This section examines the following passages:

The first miracle in Mark	1 : 21–28
The healing of Simon's mother-in-law	1 : 29–31
The healing of many people	1 : 32–34 3 : 7–12
Another summary of Jesus' healings	6 : 53–56
Jesus heals a man with leprosy	1 : 40–45
Jesus heals a paralysed man	2 : 1–12
Jesus heals a man with a paralysed hand	3 : 1–6

The first miracle in Mark

READ MARK 1 : 21–28

This takes place in the synagogue in Capernaum, where Jesus taught. He probably preached the sermon, as any adult male could do. His teaching was 'new' and 'with authority', unlike that of the teachers of the Law or **scribes**. The scribes spent their time studying the Torah and trying to apply it to everyday life. Many of them were also Pharisees, though some were Sadducees.

Jews in Jesus' time believed in demons, and thought that they caused illness. Some have suggested the man in Mark's story here was mentally ill. This may be true, but it is not the point Mark is trying to make. Jesus defeats the demon by exorcizing it. This defeat of the evil powers shows that the Kingdom has arrived.

The demon recognizes Jesus, but he orders it to be silent. The theme of Jesus not allowing news of his identity to be spread is common in Mark. He also refuses to let people say who he is in public: they are not to go around saying he is the Messiah. This theme is called the **Messianic Secret**. Various ideas have been suggested as to why Jesus does this. A good explanation is that he did not want people to get too excited. If they went around saying he was the Messiah, they might think the final showdown with the Romans was about to start. Jesus needed to teach his disciples and others what being the Messiah meant. Only then could they call him 'Messiah'.

The healing of Simon's mother-in-law

READ MARK 1 : 29–31

This story may originally have come from Simon Peter himself. Jesus does not perform his miracles for show: this one takes place in private. As with the other healings, it shows Jesus' compassion and care. When she is cured, Peter's mother-in-law begins to wait on Jesus and his disciples. Mark may be hinting that, just as she served Jesus at table, Christians should serve Jesus in their lives.

If Mark thinks the fever was caused by a demon, he does not say so.

The healing of many people

READ MARK 1 : 32–34
3 : 7–12

Another summary of Jesus' healings

READ MARK 6 : 53–56

The summaries of healing miracles show the sort of thing Mark thought Jesus did. Jesus heals a large number of people, showing that he has compassion and that the Kingdom is coming. Again, he refuses to let the demons identify him.

The people healed have come from all over Israel and from outside: some are Gentiles. That they, too, are cured shows they are also included in the Kingdom.

Jesus' power is so great that the people in the third summary only have to touch the edge of his cloak to be cured.

Jesus heals a man with leprosy

READ MARK 1 : 40–45

The Torah said people with leprosy were outside God's chosen people. They were ceremonially impure, and they had to stay away from everyone else. People were so afraid of the disease that they classed many skin complaints as 'leprosy', to be on the safe side. It is therefore possible that the man in this story did not have proper leprosy.

Jesus cures the man by touching him and by a word of command. His power to heal comes from his own authority: it is not magic. Touching a leper would have been very shocking: he risked catching the disease and would also have become ceremonially impure, according to the Torah. Jesus is moved by 'pity' (some early Greek copies of Mark say he is moved by 'anger': anger that the leper had suffered so much). He tells the man to go and make the sacrifice laid down by the Torah, and to show himself to the priest. The priest would check that he was cured. This allowed him back into society—a miracle with follow-up care as well! The story ends with a repeat of the Messianic Secret theme. Despite Jesus' command to the man to be quiet, the news spreads fast.

People with leprosy were outcasts from Judaism, but they are acceptable to Jesus. The Kingdom is open to them, too.

Jesus heals a paralysed man

READ MARK 2 : 1–12

A very vivid story. The flat roofs in Israel were made from mud plastered over branches, so it would be easy to dig through them.

People thought sin sometimes caused illness, so Jesus says the man's sins are forgiven. Perhaps the man thought he was ill because he was being punished by God. If so, Jesus' words would have been a great reassurance. The arrival of the Kingdom brings forgiveness.

Yet only God could forgive sins. That was why Jesus' words appeared blasphemous to the scribes. (It is not clear whether these scribes or teachers of the Law were Pharisees or Sadducees.) Jesus tries to show them that what he says is true. Saying 'Your sins are forgiven' is no harder than saying, 'Get up, pick up your mat and walk.' (To the Jews, these would have meant more or less the same thing.) He shows this is true by telling the man to take up his mat and go home—and the man does just that.

Note:

▷ Although the paralysed man's faith is not mentioned, the faith of his friends is important. This faith forms a kind of friendship with Jesus. All the miracles in Mark come about because faith already exists. The scribes do not have this faith in Jesus.

▷ Jesus does something only God can do: he forgives sins. Mark thus hints at who Jesus really is.

▷ Jesus is in conflict with the authorities. Already, there is a hint of the opposition that will lead to Jesus' death.

Jesus calls himself the **Son of Man** in this story. This is a difficult title. It is certainly the title Jesus preferred to 'Messiah'. In the Old Testament, 'son of man' could mean just 'human being'. So Jesus could have meant simply 'this man' or 'I'. But in the Old Testament book of Daniel, Daniel has a vision of 'someone like a son of man', who was given power by God. Later Jewish books, not in the Old Testament, said this Son of Man was someone from heaven whom God would send to judge people. But we do not know whether these later books were written before or after the time of Jesus. We certainly have no evidence that 'Son of Man' was just another name for the Messiah.

Perhaps Jesus chose the title because it was not so loaded. If he called himself 'Son of Man' instead of 'Messiah', people would not automatically think he was going to start a war with Rome.

In Mark, Jesus uses the title in three ways:

1. The Son of Man has **authority on earth** to forgive sins and he is Lord of the Sabbath (2 : 10, 28).

2. The Son of Man must **suffer, die and rise again**. This is the most important idea: there are lots of references to it (8 : 31; 9 : 9, 12, 31; 10 : 33, 45; 14 : 21, 41).

3. The Son of Man will **return**. Jesus will come back at the end of time (8 : 38; 13 : 26; 14 : 62).

We can see, then, that the 'Son of Man' title as Jesus used it sums up his life and work very well.

Jesus heals a man with a paralysed hand
READ MARK 3 : 1–6

Jewish laws allowed people to be healed on the Sabbath (the Jewish holy day). But this was only if life was in danger. The man in this story has a withered or paralysed hand, but he is not actually dying. The people who are waiting to see whether Jesus would do something wrong are the Pharisees from the previous story (the controversy over the Sabbath corn incident).

Jesus puts human need above religious rules. The coming of the Kingdom means that the old rules are no longer so important. The importance of Jesus' healing on the Sabbath is not that it breaks the Law. Its importance is that it shows the Kingdom has come.

The Pharisees meet with the Herodians ('Herod's party') to discuss how to destroy Jesus. Again, we have a reference early on in the Gospel to his death. We know practically nothing about the Herodians. Presumably, they were the supporters of Herod Antipas, the ruler of Galilee. The Pharisees thought very little of Herod. If they were willing to meet with his followers, they were getting very anxious.

Jesus calms a storm
READ MARK 4 : 35–41

This is one of the 'nature miracles', so called because they show Jesus' power over the forces of nature. The other nature miracles are the walking on the water, the feeding of the five thousand, the feeding of the four thousand and the cursing of the fig-tree.

Lake Galilee is still a stormy place. Yet the meaning of the story is more than Jesus simply stopping a violent storm:

● It shows **who Jesus is**.
God is shown to have power over water in the Old Testament. He parted the waters of the Red Sea to allow his people through when they fled from Egypt (Exodus 14). In the psalms, sailors in trouble called on God, and 'he calmed the raging storm, and the waves became quiet' (Psalm 107 : 29). The Jews believed that God controlled the weather. So, **Jesus behaves as though he is God**.
When God did something extraordinary in the Old Testament, people were said to be frightened. For example, when God gave Moses the Ten Commandments, the people 'trembled with fear' at the signs of God's appearing on the mountain. So, **the disciples were afraid because they were seeing God at work**.

● It shows Mark's readers **how to live**. Christians in distress should trust in Jesus' power to save them, not panic as the disciples did. If Mark's first readers were being persecuted by Nero, they should trust in Christ even in the face of death.

It is interesting that Mark is not afraid to show the disciples in a bad light. They are annoyed with Jesus here for sleeping, and they have very little faith in him.

The walking on the water
READ MARK 6 : 45–52

Again, the story hints at who Jesus is by mentioning his power over the water and the disciples' fear. See the notes on *Jesus calms a storm*.

In the Old Testament, God is also pictured as walking over the sea in Psalm 77 : 19:
'You walked through the waves;
you crossed the deep sea.'

Jesus is said to be about to 'pass by' the disciples. These words are also found in the Old Testament: God 'passed by' Moses and Elijah in the books of Exodus and 1 Kings. Jesus also calls out to his disciples, 'It is I.' The Greek words Mark uses here are simply, 'I am', which is what God calls himself in Exodus 3 : 14. So, once again, **Jesus behaves as though he is God**.

Some have attempted to explain away the story by saying Jesus was walking on a reef, or had built a raft. Neither of these are very convincing. Others suggest it was made up to fit in with the Old Testament. Still others point out that if God made the universe, he is not going to find it hard to make Jesus walk on water!

The feeding miracles had pointed to Jesus' identity. That is why the disciples were said not to understand about the 'loaves' (the Good News Bible makes this clearer by saying 'they had not understood the real meaning of the feeding of the five thousand'). The disciples did not work out who Jesus was from the feeding miracles, and they still cannot grasp it.

The madman in the tombs
READ MARK 5 : 1–20

Another exorcism story, very vividly told. The man is possessed by as many demons as there are soldiers in a Roman legion. Hence he gives his name as Legion or Mob. The miracle takes place at Gerasa or Gadara (different Greek copies of Mark give both names). Neither of these places is very near Lake Galilee, which shows that Mark's geography is not very good. However, it is important that they are both *Gentile* towns. The man Jesus heals is a Gentile. Gentiles are admitted into the Kingdom.

The madman is chained up in a region near some tombs, one of the locations where it was believed demons lived. Mark thinks the demons give him the supernatural insight to recognize Jesus. Jesus asks him his name: it was believed that an exorcist could cast out a demon more easily if he knew his name. The destruction of the pigs demonstrates that the demons have been cast out.

After he is cured, the man spreads the message about Jesus throughout the region of the Ten Towns ('the Decapolis').

Some scholars have suggested that a miracle story about Jesus has been mixed up with a folk tale about some pigs. This is possible, but there is no real evidence. It could be said that the man needed proof that he was cured, so Jesus somehow made the pigs stampede, or they ran off when they were frightened by the madman.

Jairus' daughter and the woman who touched Jesus' cloak
READ MARK 5 : 21–43

Both these stories involve females. Women and girls were considered to be second-class citizens in the Jewish world of Jesus' day. However, Jesus does not share this attitude. If someone needs help, it is given. It does not matter whether that person is male or female.

The woman who touched Jesus' cloak had a menstrual problem, or some infection that produced similar symptoms. This would have made her unclean according to the Torah, but her faith, Jesus says, has 'saved' her (this is what the Greek says). She is completely cured, in body, mind and spirit. She is now one of the family, a 'daughter' of Jesus and a member of the Kingdom of God.

Jairus organized the worship in the local synagogue. He too has faith in Jesus, who takes Peter, James and John with him. These three disciples are the only ones present at some other important events, including the Transfiguration and the visit to Gethsemane. This is the only miracle story in Mark in which Jesus raises the dead. It is therefore very important:

● Only God has power over death. In the Old Testament, Elijah prays that God will bring a dead boy back to life, and God does so. But here Jesus does not pray first: he does it himself. Again, he behaves as though he is God.

● Jesus' raising the little girl from death is a shadow of what is to come at the end of Mark: Jesus will himself rise from the dead. (However, Jairus' daughter was brought back to normal life, whereas Jesus was raised to a new kind of life.)

● The story reminds the readers that Jesus will save them from death as well. Christians' relationship with Jesus in the Kingdom will, they believe, continue after death.

The feeding of the five thousand
READ MARK 6 : 30–44

The Old Testament says God fed his people in the desert with food from heaven called manna. Moses was their leader then. The feeding of the five thousand also takes place in a desert. One Jewish teacher (rabbi) said that the Messiah would feed people miraculously as Moses had done. In the Old Testament, too, Elijah's successor Elisha fed one hundred men with twenty small loaves (2 Kings 4 : 42–44). So, the story shows:

1. Jesus is the Messiah who feeds the people as Moses had done.

2. Jesus fulfils the Law, represented by Moses, and the prophets, represented by Elisha.

3. Jesus behaves as though he is God. Like God, he produces food miraculously.

The story also looks forward to the Last Supper and to the Messianic Banquet. (The Messianic Banquet was a picture of the Kingdom as a big celebration meal.) The Messiah here hosts a meal for a lot of people, just as he will at the Messianic Banquet. He gives the people bread, just as he will give the disciples the bread of his body at the Last Supper, and the Church—Mark's church, and the Church today—will repeat his actions in the Eucharist.

Some scholars have suggested that the whole story has been invented, or that the numbers of people or the amount of food has been exaggerated, or that people just shared their packed lunch, and this was mistaken for a miracle. Not everyone finds these 'explanations' very convincing. Certainly Mark thought he was writing about a miracle, and a very important one at that. He gives us two versions of it.

The feeding of the four thousand
READ MARK 8 : 1–10

The same points should be made about this miracle as about the feeding of the five thousand. It is almost certainly a different version of the same story.

The feeding of the four thousand takes place in the region of the Ten Towns (Decapolis). This was a Gentile area. The feeding of the five thousand took place in a Jewish area. So,

▷ the feeding of the four thousand shows the bread of life being given to the Gentiles
▷ the feeding of the five thousand shows the bread of life being given to the Jews.

Both Jews and Gentiles take part in a meal which is a shadow of the Messianic Banquet. Both are therefore included in the Kingdom of God.

Jesus heals a Gentile woman's daughter
READ MARK 7 : 24–30

Most Jews in Jesus' time thought women were second-class citizens. They would have thought Gentile women were even worse! Jesus once again treats people as people, regardless of their sex or race.

Jesus says it is unfair to take bread from the children (Jews) and throw it to the dogs (Gentiles). (He was certainly not being insulting—that would be completely out of character—but most likely joking ironically.) The woman from Syro-Phoenicia is very sharp, and replies that even the dogs under the table get the children's scraps. Her faith is great, and Jesus cures her daughter. It is interesting that he does so from a distance.

The woman calls Jesus **Lord** ('Sir'). These are two ways of translating the Greek word *kyrios* into English. Any man with authority could be called 'kyrios'. It was also the name used for God in the Greek translation of the Old Testament. The title shows that Jesus has authority, and also hints at who he really is.

Jesus heals a deaf-mute

READ MARK 7 : 31–37

This is another Gentile healing. There are other stories of healers in the ancient world who used saliva in their cures. (This may be why the other Gospels omit this story.) Mark gives Jesus' words of healing in Aramaic, the language Jesus spoke (see also 5 : 41). He translates them for his non-Jewish readers. He may have got them from Peter, and may include them for the benefit of Christian healers who believed they needed to use such words.

The passage is similar to Isaiah's prediction that when the Messiah comes,
'the blind will be able to see,
and the deaf will hear.'

Jesus heals a blind man

READ MARK 8 : 22–26

This miracle is very similar to the healing of the deaf-mute. Again, the same points need to be noted. In both, the man's friends ask for Jesus' help, he uses saliva, and tries to keep his Messiahship secret. This story is unusual because the cure happens gradually, not immediately.

Jesus opens a blind man's eyes. In the stories which follow this one, he opens his disciples' eyes to who he really is. The next stories are Peter's declaration about Jesus, and the Transfiguration.

Jesus heals an epileptic boy

READ MARK 9 : 14–29

The boy's symptoms suggest that he has epilepsy, which was attributed to a very violent demon. Jesus performs a miracle in healing the boy—it is interesting to note that there is no cure for epilepsy, even today.

A major theme of the story is the need for faith. Here, the teachers of the Law (scribes) have no faith. The disciples need it: they have been given the authority to heal people, but Mark probably thinks they cannot do so here because of their lack of faith. The boy's father needs greater faith. His outburst in verse 24 has provided an apt prayer for Christians in difficult times. It may have been especially important to Mark's own church, if it was persecuted by Nero.

Jesus says only prayer can cast out this sort of demon. Mark may have included this comment as an instruction for Christian healers.

Jesus heals blind Bartimaeus

READ MARK 10 : 46–50

Jericho was only fifteen miles from Jerusalem. Jesus and the disciples are on a journey, and now very near to the place where he will die. It is the disciples who are really blind, not Bartimaeus. This healing follows on from James' and John's question. The disciples still do not understand what Jesus' mission means. They need to follow Jesus, just as Bartimaeus follows him on the road. That road leads to Jerusalem and to Golgotha.

The title **Son of David** for Jesus is only found twice in Mark: here, and in the passage with the question about the Messiah (12 : 35–37). David was the great Jewish king who, a thousand years before Jesus, was promised by God that one of his descendants or 'sons' would always rule (2 Samuel 7 : 12–13). 'Son of David' means 'descendant of David' and was another name for the Messiah.

The cursing of the fig-tree

READ MARK 11 : 12–14
20–25

Some find this story totally out of character, and cannot believe Jesus did it. Others have suggested that a parable told by Jesus has been turned into a story about him. Mark probably thinks of it as an acted prophecy: a visual aid. Some of the Old Testament prophets performed symbolic actions to get a message across, as Jesus does here.

The fig-tree in the Old Testament was used as a symbol for Israel (Jeremiah 8 : 13). So the story's interpretation is as follows:

● Jesus is hungry for figs.
   God is 'hungry' for the 'fruit' of good actions and true religion from Israel.

● It is not the right time for figs.
   It is not the right time for God to expect 'fruit' from his people.

- No one will ever eat fruit from the tree again.
  The fig-tree of Israel is also barren. The new Israel of the Church has replaced it.

- The fig-tree dies.
  The time of Israel as God's people is over.

Mark places some of Jesus' teaching on prayer after this story. This shows that he also sees the miracle as a sign of the power of faith. The idea that you can move mountains if you have enough faith is not to be taken literally. It means that you will be able to overcome problems and hardships that seemed impossible. God will always answer people's prayers, but people will also have to forgive others when they pray. If they do not, they cannot receive forgiveness for their own sins.

Section 6: Controversy stories

This section examines the following passages:

The question about fasting	**2 : 18–22**
The Sabbath corn	**2 : 23–28**
Jesus and Beelzebul	**3 : 20–30**
What makes a person unclean?	**7 : 1–23**
The Pharisees ask for a sign; the yeast of the Pharisees and of Herod	**8 : 11–21**
Jesus' teaching on divorce	**10 : 1–12**
The cleansing of the Temple	**11 : 15–19**
The question about authority	**11 : 27–33**
The allegory of the vineyard	**12 : 1–12**
The question about paying taxes	**12 : 13–17**
The question about the resurrection of the dead	**12 : 18–27**
The greatest commandment	**12 : 28–34**
The question about the Messiah	**12 : 35–37**
Jesus warns against the teachers of the Law (scribes)	**12 : 37b–40**

There are two other relevant passages, which are studied under the heading 'Miracles':

Jesus heals a paralysed man	**2 : 1–12**
Jesus heals a man with a paralysed hand	**3 : 1–6**

The question about fasting

READ MARK 2 : 18–22

Strict Jews in Jesus' time fasted every Monday and Thursday from 6 a.m. to 6 p.m. This may explain why the disciples of John the Baptist and of the Pharisees were fasting.

The people who came to ask Jesus about this may well have been Pharisees. Jesus says it is not the right time for fasting. It is a time to rejoice, just as the guests rejoice at a wedding. In the Old Testament, God was sometimes thought of as Israel's bridegroom. Mark again hints at Jesus' identity. The Old Testament prophet Hosea said that Israel's marriage to God had broken down so badly that there had been a divorce. But Hosea also predicted a new marriage. Jesus is the bridegroom in this new marriage between God and human beings.

A wedding feast also suggests the Messianic Banquet, the picture of the Kingdom of God as a celebration meal.

The bridegroom will be taken away: Jesus will die. After that, his followers will fast. Jesus uses two images or parables to show that the new does not mix with the old. The Kingdom has replaced the old order of Judaism:

> ▷ it is no good patching an old coat with new cloth;
> ▷ wine which needs to ferment cannot be stored in brittle, used wineskins: if it is, the skins will burst.

The Sabbath corn
READ MARK 2 : 23–28

Jews were allowed to pick food from fields or vineyards, so the disciples are not stealing. The Pharisees objected to it because the Law forbade work, including reaping, on the Sabbath (Exodus 34 : 21). Their interpretation of the Law is strict, as usual. Jesus reminds them why God gave the Jews the Torah: to help them. After all, King David broke the Law by taking holy bread to eat when his men were hungry, and David was a great man of God. Human need comes before religious laws. Mark probably thinks that the Kingdom sits rather uneasily with Judaism.

Jesus says the Sabbath was made for people's benefit, not the other way round. He has the authority to say this because the Son of Man is Lord of the Sabbath. This outlook would have outraged these Pharisees. It was utterly alien to their way of thinking.

Jesus and Beelzebul
READ MARK 3 : 20–30

Jesus' family think he is 'beside himself'. The teachers of the Law (scribes) go further and say he is possessed by a demon. They think this gives him the power to perform exorcisms. This idea is not just wicked, it is also stupid. If Jesus did use the Devil's power to drive out demons, then the forces of evil would be fighting among themselves, and God would still be winning.

Jesus' miracles are in fact signs of the Kingdom. The Devil, the 'strong man', is being tied up by the miracles and is being overthrown. The scribes' accusation comes very close to saying that something God does is not good at all, but evil. This sort of blindness makes forgiveness impossible. If people cannot recognize goodness when they see it, how can they turn to God and find forgiveness?

What makes a person unclean?
READ MARK 7 : 1–23

Mark explains the Pharisees' rules on ceremonial washing, for the benefit of his Gentile readers. The Pharisees thought these traditions were nearly as important as the Torah itself. It is worth taking careful note of what Mark says about them (verses 3–4).

The Pharisees expect Jesus' disciples to wash their hands in the traditional way. (This was to do with ritual, not with hygiene.) Jesus says they are the hypocrites of whom Isaiah spoke. They have fallen into the trap of thinking their own tradition is as important as what God wants. This can be seen in Corban laws. One of the Ten Commandments is 'honour your father and mother'. This would obviously cover looking after them, which could cost money. People could get out of spending money on their needy parents, however, by making a solemn oath that it 'belonged to God': it was **Corban**. They broke God's Law by taking advantage of a man-made rule.

Jesus' words in verse 15 are a real bombshell. The Pharisees are completely wrong. *Nothing* that goes into someone can make them 'unclean' or ceremonially impure. God is not really bothered about how people wash their hands, or whether they keep strict kosher rules. What really matters is what comes from the heart: the evil things that come from within.

One of the biggest issues that faced the early Church was whether Gentile Christians had to keep the Torah. Mark's church was probably Gentile. Stories like this were useful in the debate. Since Mark includes this account, it is likely that the debate was still going on when he was writing.

The Pharisees ask for a sign; the yeast of the Pharisees and of Herod

READ MARK 8 : 11–21

Throughout his work Jesus has been giving signs by performing miracles. Yet the Pharisees still want a sign. They refuse to see what has been staring them in the face, and will not believe. Jesus refuses to do a miracle solely for their benefit. Even if he did, they would probably still not accept it!

The next few verses (14–21) are difficult. Jesus warns the disciples against the 'yeast' of the Pharisees and of Herod. The rabbis sometimes used the word 'yeast' to mean evil intentions or ideas. Jesus is warning the Twelve against the Pharisees' teaching, and perhaps against the followers of Herod Antipas. The disciples think he is complaining because they have forgotten their packed lunches! They ought to know better by now: they have seen the two feeding miracles, so they should realize that they can rely on Jesus.

It is difficult to be sure why Jesus reminds the disciples about the number of baskets. It may be because twelve is a number associated with the Jews (twelve tribes of Israel). Seven is a 'Gentile number' (there were seven deacons or church leaders in Acts to look after the Gentiles; the Gentile world was also divided into seventy countries, and 7 x 10 = 70!). Both Jews and Gentiles were fed by Jesus, and both were included in the Kingdom of God. Jesus drives this point home by talking about the number of baskets.

Jesus' teaching on divorce

READ MARK 10 : 1–12

The Torah did not allow a woman to divorce her husband, but a man could divorce his wife if she were 'guilty of some shameful conduct' (Deuteronomy 24 : 1). The issue was: how 'shameful' did the 'conduct' have to be?

Jews in Jesus' time were divided into two schools of thought:

▷ Some who agreed with Rabbi Shammai. 'Shameful conduct' meant 'adultery' and nothing else.

▷ More who agreed with Rabbi Hillel. 'Shameful conduct' meant anything the man did not like. A man could therefore divorce his wife if she burnt his dinner!

Divorce for a woman was a terrible disgrace. Given all this, it is hardly surprising that Jesus is so strict. The Torah allowed divorce only because human beings were pig-headed. Yet when God created them, they were designed for marriage. There should therefore be no divorce. Re-marriage is adultery. (Jesus mentions women divorcing their husbands because this was allowed by Roman law.) The women of Jesus' time should be allowed to live in love, security and respect.

Christians today have differing views on divorce:

● Some think it is always wrong. The Roman Catholic Church does not recognize divorce at all. However, it does allow 'annulment'. This is a declaration, in certain cases, that a marriage never took place.

● Others allow divorce, even though nobody thinks it is ideal. In Matthew's Gospel, Jesus does seem to allow it if adultery has taken place, and Jesus says his teaching on marriage 'does not apply to everyone, but only to those to whom God has given it' (Matthew 19 : 11). Some would argue that taking a hard line with people in difficult and distressing circumstances is not the best way to help them.

The cleansing of the Temple

READ MARK 11 : 15–19

Jesus is now in Jerusalem. This incident and all the following passages are set in Holy Week, the week leading up to his death. The story is framed by the cursing of the fig-tree (see the section on *Miracles*). The theme is the same.

The Old Testament prophet Malachi had predicted that the Messiah, 'the Lord you are looking for will suddenly come to his Temple' (Malachi 3 : 1). The Temple was at the heart of Judaism. Jesus' action shows God's judgement on Israel. The house of God had been turned into a den of thieves.

▷ Animals for sacrifice had to be perfect, so traders were selling them for a big profit.

▷ Every male Jew had to pay a tax for the Temple's upkeep. This had to be paid with the special Temple coinage. Business was good for the money-changers, who were probably making a lot of money.

▷ People were using the Temple, the holiest place in the world, as a short-cut.

All this was happening in the Court of the Gentiles, the only part of the Temple into which the Gentiles could go. It was a 'house of prayer for all nations' (the Gentiles), not a market or a thoroughfare!

Jesus enrages the Jewish authorities, who want him dead.

The question about authority
READ MARK 11 : 27–33

Jesus' questioners are identified as the chief priests, the teachers of the Law (scribes) and the elders. Where does Jesus' authority come from? How can a carpenter interfere with the running of the Temple? The question is a trap. If Jesus says he gets his authority from God, he could be arrested for blasphemy. If he says he behaves in a way he thinks is right, he would lose face: only a maniac would make a claim like that!

Jesus brilliantly side-steps the question, and sets one of his own. Now the authorities cannot win. If they say John's authority came from God, Jesus will ask them why they did not believe him. After all, John pointed to Jesus. If they deny that John's authority came from God, they risk a riot. Everyone thinks John was a prophet. They cannot answer Jesus, and Jesus will not answer them.

The allegory of the vineyard
READ MARK 12 : 1–12

An allegory is a type of parable in which each event or person stands for something in reality.

Foreigners often bought land in Galilee and rented it to the locals. The locals resented it. This is the background to the story.

The allegory can be explained as follows:

● The vineyard owner is God.

● The vineyard is Israel. (In the Old Testament, Isaiah uses a vineyard as a symbol for Israel.)

● The tenants are the Jewish leaders, who behave badly.

● The slaves/servants are the prophets. God wants right action and right religion from his people; the vineyard owner wants his share of the harvest. Both send messengers.

● The servants are beaten up or killed. The prophets were treated the same way.

● The vineyard owner decided to send his 'beloved son'. If the tenants do not listen to the messengers, they may listen to the son. The 'beloved son' of God is Jesus. (The voice from heaven calls him exactly that at his baptism and the Transfiguration.)

● The tenants kill the man's son. The authorities will kill Jesus.

● The owner of the vineyard will kill the tenants. God will not allow the authorities to get away with Jesus' death, although how they will be punished is not stated.

● The owner will hand the vineyard over to others. The 'others' are the Gentiles, outcasts and sinners. They are now God's people, incorporated into his Kingdom. Israel is no longer the people of God.

● Just as some builders reject a piece of stone as useless, the authorities reject Jesus as the Messiah. Yet the stone will turn out to be the most important of all. Jesus will be shown to be the Messiah.

Again, the authorities are furious, but cannot act because of the crowd.

The question about paying taxes
READ MARK 12 : 13–17

This time it is the Pharisees and the Herodians who try to trap Jesus. We know very little about the Herodians: presumably they were members of Herod's party, the supporters of Herod Antipas.

The Jews hated paying Roman taxes. If Jesus tells them not to pay the tax, he will be popular with them. Yet the Romans could arrest him as a traitor. If he says they should pay the tax, people will stop following him. No Messiah would say that! Jesus again gives a brilliant reply. The coin showed Caesar's head, it was his property. 'Pay the Emperor what belongs to the Emperor, and pay God what belongs to God.'

Some Christians have taken this to mean that Christians should always obey the government, though this is not what Jesus actually says. Others think he is implying that doing what God wants is more important than doing what human beings want. If there is a clash, Christians should obey God, not human authority.

The question about the resurrection of the dead
READ MARK 12 : 18–27

The **Sadducees**, who asked this question, were a small, aristocratic group. Many of them were wealthy, and they did not want trouble with the Romans which might affect their power. Many were priests in the Temple. They accepted only those ideas which were in the Torah, so they did not believe in angels or the Messiah. Nor did they believe in life after death ('the resurrection', which should not be confused with the resurrection of Jesus). Their question here is designed to make belief in the resurrection look silly. It is based on a law in Deuteronomy. This says that if a married man has no children and dies, his brother must marry the widow so that the dead man's family line will continue. So, they ask, what happens if there are seven brothers, and none of them have children? If there is life after death ('the resurrection'), whose wife will she be?

Jesus does not go into detail, but he makes it clear that the dead will rise to life, and says that there will then be no marriage, as people will be 'like angels', though it is not clear what this means. As the Sadducees only accept the Torah, this is what Jesus quotes from. In Exodus, God spoke to Moses from a burning bush. God said, 'I am' (not 'I was') 'the God of Abraham, the God of Isaac, and the God of Jacob.' Abraham, Isaac and Jacob were long dead, but God's words imply that somehow they are still alive.

Christians believe in life after death. The New Testament seems to have two main ideas about it, as do Christians today:

1. After death, people go straight to heaven or hell—into God's presence, or totally separated from him. (The Roman Catholic Church's official line is that only very few people are good enough to go straight to heaven. Others first go to a 'place' called purgatory. Many Roman Catholics think of purgatory not so much as a place, but as the pain of being separated from worldly things.)

2. When people die, they will have to 'wait', to 'rest in peace', until God ends the universe (although it is difficult to know how time can have any meaning after death, so these two ideas may not be so different after all). Then the dead will rise and be judged. God will make a 'new heaven and a new earth' (Revelation 21:1). The New Testament is clear that people will have some sort of a body after death: they will not just be souls.

Christianity teaches that it is enough to trust in God and in his promises. God is too good and loving to let his friends be destroyed in death. However, he does not provide people with information about the furniture of heaven or the temperature of hell!

The greatest commandment
READ MARK 12 : 28–34

The teacher of the Law (scribe) is not trying to trap Jesus. He is genuinely interested in Jesus' answer to a favourite problem of the Rabbis. Which of the commandments in the Torah sums up all the others?

The command to 'love God' is from the beginning of the prayer called the Shema, from Deuteronomy 6 : 4–5. In Jesus' time, it was recited three times a day. It was written out and placed in boxes (phylacteries) strapped to the head and wrist during prayer times. Similar boxes were placed on the doorposts of Jewish homes. Both practices continue among Orthodox Jews today.

The command to 'love your neighbour as you love yourself' is from Leviticus 19 : 18. Originally, 'neighbour' meant 'fellow Israelite': here, it means 'everybody'.

Jesus was the first Jewish teacher to sum up the Torah with these two commandments.

As the scribe agrees with Jesus, he is not far from the Kingdom of God.

Mark's readers may have found this story useful in the debate over whether Gentile Christians have to keep the Torah. If they loved God and loved their neighbours, did they really have to keep the rest of the Torah?

The question about the Messiah

READ MARK 12 : 35–37

Jesus now asks a question. David, who was believed to have written the psalms, calls the Christ 'My Lord'. So how can the scribes say the Christ is the Son of David? Surely he is more than that?

Some scholars have suggested that Jesus was not in fact descended from David. If this is right, stories like this one try to get round the problem. (The Jews believed the Messiah had to be descended from David, but Jesus was not!) However, the New Testament is clear that Jesus was descended from David. If this is correct, Jesus is saying here that the Christ is *more* than the Son of David. (He certainly is not going to be a warrior at the head of a Jewish empire, as David was!)

Jesus warns against the teachers of the Law (scribes)

READ MARK 12 : 37B–40

Jesus warns the crowd against the teachers of the Law:

1. They like walking around in long shawls (talliths), which were usually worn for prayer. They either have extra-large versions, or wear them all the time, or have extra large tassels on them. The point is that they like to be noticed. (The Greek here can also mean that they like to walk up and down in the Temple's covered walkways—'porticoes'.)

2. They want people's respect, but do not deserve it.

3. They want the best seats in the synagogue and at dinner parties.

4. They make a big to-do about praying, but extort money from needy people. Such behaviour can only earn them the greatest condemnation.

Section 7: The end of the world (the apocalyptic discourse)

READ MARK 13 : 1–37

This section examines chapter 13. It is not a particularly popular section for examination questions, but it is still worth knowing.

Both the Jews and the early Christians believed that a day would come when God would wind up history. On that day, the good would be rewarded and the wicked punished. Apocalyptic books were written about what would happen. ('Apocalyptic' comes from a Greek word meaning 'to uncover/reveal secrets'.) Examples of such books from the Bible include Daniel and Revelation. Chapter 13 of Mark gives Jesus' teaching about the end of the world. It is often called 'the Little Apocalypse', although its language and ideas are not as extreme or strange as other apocalyptic books. How much of it goes back to Jesus himself is debated by scholars. It is addressed to Peter, James and John, the inner group of the disciples. Jesus' teaching about the end is as follows:

● The Temple will be destroyed. (The Romans did destroy it in AD70.)

● People will come and claim falsely to speak for Jesus, saying 'I am he!'

● There will be wars, rumours of wars, earthquakes and famines. The Christians must not get too excited: these are not signs that the end will be very soon.

They are like the first pangs of childbirth: they show that something is going to happen, but not the precise time.

- Christians will suffer for their faith
  - ▷ before a court;
  - ▷ before rulers and kings;
  - ▷ by being put to death by members of their own family;
  - ▷ by being hated by everyone.

But there are promises, too:
- ▷ The Holy Spirit will speak for the Christians when they are in court. God will guide them in what to say.
- ▷ Whoever holds out to the end will be saved. This may fit in with the situation in Mark's church, which may have been persecuted by Nero. Christians have been persecuted for their faith throughout history.

- The gospel must be preached to all nations (Gentiles) before the end will come. This idea has inspired many missionaries.

- When the 'abomination of desolation' ('the awful horror') is set up, people in Judea must flee to the hills. Escape will be hard for pregnant women and for those with young children, and harder still in winter.
  The verses about running away to the mountains seem to be talking about fleeing from a siege. The Romans besieged Jerusalem in AD70. The events of this siege may be what the 'abomination of desolation' means.
  Others have suggested the abomination refers to the coming of the Antichrist (the devil or his representative) at the end of the world. Or it could refer to the attempt made by the Emperor Caligula to set up his statue in the Temple in AD40.

- God has shortened the days of suffering before the end. This is because of his concern for his chosen people.

- Imposters claiming to be prophets or even to be Jesus will try to dazzle people and lead them astray. Even if they perform miracles, the Christians should not believe them.

- The final and full arrival of the Kingdom of God will be when Jesus returns. The idea of the Son of Man coming on clouds is best understood as picture language.

- When a fig-tree puts out its leaves, it shows that summer is near. When the disciples see these things happening, they should realize that the end is near. The events will take place before all those now living have died. Mark 13 now seems, after all, to be saying that the end will be soon. Perhaps a different source is being used here.

- Jesus' words will never pass away.

- No one, not even Jesus, knows exactly when the end will come. Only God the Father knows. The Christians should not try to work out a timetable for the end. The 'servants' (Christians) do not know when their master will come back. So they must keep awake and be ready for him.

Section 8: Jesus' Passion and resurrection

This section examines the following passages:

The triumphal entry

READ MARK 11 : 1–11

Jesus enters Jerusalem, and the Passion story begins. 'Passion' comes from a Greek word meaning 'to suffer'.

The people greet Jesus as the Messiah. The Old Testament prophet Zechariah had predicted that the Messiah would come 'triumphant and victorious, but humble and riding on a donkey' (Zechariah 9 : 9). Jesus fulfils this prophecy. Victorious kings used to ride war horses in processions. Jesus rides on a colt because he has come in peace.

The crowd's greeting, 'Blessed is he who comes in the name of the Lord!' was the normal greeting for any pilgrim who arrived in Jerusalem. Passover time was near, and people were flocking to the holy city. Yet they also recognize that the Kingdom is near.

The word 'Hosanna' originally meant 'save now'. By Jesus' time, it had become a traditional shout of praise.

Jesus' triumphal entry into Jerusalem is remembered by Christians today on Palm Sunday, the first day of Holy Week. Holy Week is the last week of Lent, the forty-day period which prepares Christians for Easter. On Palm Sunday, Christians often re-enact Jesus' entry into Jerusalem, usually during the Eucharist. There may be a procession, with palm branches or palm crosses (crosses made from palm leaves). The hymns and readings remember the welcome the crowd gave Jesus, and the rest of his Passion.

The plot against Jesus

READ MARK 14 : 1–2

Passover recalled how God rescued the Jews from the Egyptians. He appointed Moses as their leader, and brought them through the Red Sea to the promised land of Israel. The Festival of Unleavened Bread lasted for seven days after the Passover. It marked the beginning of the barley harvest. This name also reminded the people that, when God brought them out of Egypt, there was not even time to wait for their bread to rise.

Every good Jew wanted to spend at least one Passover in Jerusalem. The city was crammed with pilgrims. Patriotic feelings ran high. People with Zealot sympathies might be hoping that God would save them from the Romans, just as he had saved them from the Egyptians. So the chief priests and scribes are afraid of a riot, even though they still want Jesus arrested.

From now on, the story runs without a break. Mark spends a great deal of time on the Passion, which shows it was important to him and to his readers.

Why was Jesus' death so important to the early Christians?

Jesus died at Passover time. The Passover was seen as the foundation of the covenant or agreement between God and his people. The Jews agreed to keep the Torah—God's Law—and God agreed to be their special God. They kept God's covenant by worshipping him. Sacrifice in the Temple was an important part of this worship. It was believed many sacrifices could take away sin.

The Christians came to realize that Jesus' death was like a sacrifice. But it was a perfect sacrifice. It did not take away only some sins of the Jews: it took away the sins of the whole world. God once saved his people from Egypt and gave them a covenant. Now, he had raised Jesus from the dead, and had therefore saved everyone from death itself. He was offering everyone a new relationship with him: a new covenant.

Christians today still believe this. No matter how hard people try, they will never be as good as they ought to be. If the world were judged in a sort of cosmic law court, no one would do very well. Yet God did not want that to happen. The love and obedience Jesus had in dying can somehow make up for everything human beings do wrong. It puts everything right between people and God, and is therefore called the atonement (at-one-ment).

Christians believe that people need to receive the benefits of the atonement. Protestant Christians believe that people only need faith to enable them to share in Jesus' saving work. Catholic Christians emphasize more than Protestants the need for 'good works'—loving God and our neighbour.

It is clear what the atonement is, but not precisely how it works. People use different models—picture language—to help them understand it. The idea of Jesus' death as a sacrifice is one model. There are other models, too:

- If you were unable to offer a sacrifice to show you were sorry for wrongdoing, you could pay money instead. Jesus' death acts like this money, and it is Jesus who pays it on everyone's behalf.

- People are slaves to sin. Jesus' death releases or redeems them from their slavery.

- People owe God a 'fine' as punishment for their sin. Jesus' death pays the fine.

- In Jesus' death, God enters into the suffering of the world. By his resurrection, Jesus offers people a way through that suffering.

It is important to remember that these are models. Their picture language helps us to understand the atonement, but they all fall short of a complete picture.

Jesus' anointing
READ MARK 14 : 3–9

Jesus mixes with outcasts right to the end. Here he is in the house of Simon the leper. Lepers were ceremonially unclean—barred from worship or contact with God's people.

It was polite to pour a little perfume on guests who arrived at your house. Yet the woman is not Jesus' host, and she uses a whole jar of very expensive perfume, showing how important Jesus is to her. The meaning of this action is twofold:

1. When people died, their bodies were anointed with perfume. The jars were not re-used: they were broken, and the pieces were placed in the tomb. The woman anoints Jesus for burial.

2. 'Christ' and 'Messiah' both mean 'the anointed one'. It is now that the Christ is anointed. Yet it is not Elijah who does so: it is a woman. Women were considered to be second-class citizens in Jesus' day, yet a woman is here given the highest honour. And Jesus is anointed as Messiah when he is about to suffer and die.

Jesus rebukes the other guests. Being good to the poor is important, but it does not rule out other generous actions.

Judas
READ MARK 14 : 10–11

Judas' offer enables the chief priests to arrest Jesus quietly, without fear of a riot.

It may be that Judas betrayed Jesus because he was a Zealot and was disappointed when Jesus did not turn out to be the sort of Messiah he wanted. Or he may have done it for the money.

The Last Supper
READ MARK 14 : 12–31

Jesus' instructions to the disciples about finding a room show that he is in control of what was happening. It is not clear whether Jesus has arranged in advance with the man carrying the water jar, or whether Mark thinks it is a miracle. (It may have been arranged in advance: women usually carried water jars. A man carrying one looks like a pre-arranged signal.)

Mark believes that the Last Supper was a Passover meal. This was—and still is—the meal eaten by Jews to remember the events of the first Passover, when God rescued his people from Egypt. The Angel of Death passed over the Jewish homes, whose doors were daubed with the blood of the Passover lambs, but he killed the firstborn sons of the Egyptians. In Jesus' day, the lamb for each family's meal was taken to the Temple to be slaughtered by the priests as a sacrifice, and then taken home to be cooked and eaten.

Jesus' words in verse 21 show that the whole of the Passion fulfils the Old Testament. This includes Judas' betrayal. Compare Mark's account with Psalm 41 : 9:

> *'Even my best friend, the one I trusted most,*
> *the one who shared my food,*
> *has turned against me.'*

It would have been better for Judas if he had not been born. This may mean he will go to hell, or it may refer to his death. Matthew's Gospel says that Judas was so stricken with guilt that he hanged himself. Jesus may mean it would have been better not to have been born than to suffer this.

Jesus' words and actions over the bread and wine have always stood at the heart of Christian worship.

Jesus acts as any Jewish host in taking the bread, thanking God for it, and breaking it. Yet he adds that the bread is his body. Just as the bread is broken at the Passover meal, Jesus' body will be broken on the cross.

The wine at the Passover meal symbolized the agreement or covenant between God and the Jews. Jesus takes the cup, and again thanks God. Yet he adds the extraordinary words:

> *'This is my blood which is poured out for many,*
> *my blood which seals God's covenant.'*

In the Old Testament, the prophet Jeremiah predicted that God would make a new covenant with the people, and he would forgive their sins. Jesus makes the new covenant here. The old covenant was sealed by the blood of sacrifices, especially that of the Passover lamb. The new covenant is sealed by the blood of Jesus, who is sacrificed on the cross.

When Moses sealed the first covenant, he threw the blood on the people, saying, 'This is the blood that seals the covenant which the Lord made with you' (Exodus 24 : 8). When the Jews ate the Passover lamb and were sprinkled with the blood of Moses' sacrifice, they became and remained the people of God's first covenant. Now the old sacrifices are replaced by Jesus' death. When people eat and drink at the Eucharist, they are part of God's new covenant.

Jesus will not drink wine again until he drinks the new wine of the Messianic Banquet, the Kingdom of God. So the Last Supper and the Eucharist are a foretaste of what is to come: the fellowship with Christ in heaven.

Jesus further predicts that all the disciples will fall away, as predicted in the Old Testament (he quotes from Zechariah 13 : 7). The disciples say that they will stay faithful, yet Peter is told that he will deny Jesus three times before the cock has crowed twice. The next time they will see him is after the resurrection, 'in Galilee'.

The re-enactment of the Last Supper has always been vital in Christian worship. It is called by various names: Eucharist, Mass, Holy Communion, the Lord's Supper, the Liturgy, the Breaking of Bread. All Christians agree that it calls to mind Jesus' sacrifice on the cross and the new covenant. After that, opinion divides.

The Eucharist is at the heart of the Church's worship in Catholic Christianity (Roman Catholics, Eastern Orthodox and some Anglicans—'Anglo-Catholics'). It is called the Mass, or the Liturgy by the Orthodox. It is celebrated frequently. Catholic Christians try to go to Mass every Sunday and on the great holy days of the Church's year. They believe that the bread and the wine of the Eucharist change, and become a channel of God's love—a sacrament. They still appear to be bread and wine, but really become the body and blood of the risen Jesus. Jesus becomes present in them: they are far more than a reminder of him. Each Christian receives Jesus when he or she eats his body and drinks his blood. The ritual that has grown up around the Mass emphasizes how holy it is.

The Eucharist is seen by Protestant Christianity (Evangelical Anglicans, the United Reformed Church, Baptists, Methodists, the Free Evangelical Churches) more as a commemoration or memorial of Jesus' death. It is celebrated less often than in Catholic churches. These Christians do not believe that the bread and wine change in any way; instead they symbolize Christians' unity with Christ in his death and in his resurrection. They also symbolize the fellowship between Christians. The Eucharist is often celebrated with moving simplicity in church, or in 'house groups' in people's homes.

Jesus in Gethsemane
READ MARK 14 : 32–52

There are a number of things to note about this passage:

▷ Gethsemane was an olive grove on the Mount of Olives.
▷ Jesus is genuinely terrified by death, although he has the courage to drink the 'cup' that is offered to him.
▷ Jesus calls God 'Abba' in prayer. This is the Aramaic word for 'Dad' or 'Daddy'. Jews did not use it because it was too informal. The early Christians did use it in their worship.
▷ The gang of men whom Judas brings are from the Sanhedrin, the Jewish council.
▷ Jesus is not an 'outlaw' or Zealot. He stops the scuffle.
▷ The disciples run off. They do not meet Jesus again until after he is raised from the dead.
▷ The young man who runs away naked is a curious detail. It has been suggested that he is an eyewitness from whom Mark got his information, or even that he is Mark himself.
▷ The events of this night from the Last Supper onwards are remembered by Christians on Maundy Thursday, the Thursday of Holy Week. At the Maundy Thursday Eucharist, the readings recall the night's events. There is often a vigil afterwards, which is usually held in one of the side chapels. People will pray through the night, remembering Jesus' agony in the garden as though they are watching with him.

Jesus' trial before the Sanhedrin
READ MARK 14 : 53–65

Mark presents the Sanhedrin as breaking every rule in the book in their determination to have Jesus put to death:

● The witnesses lie. They claim Jesus spoke against the Temple, saying he would destroy it. (Jesus had in fact predicted its destruction, but had not said that he would do it.) The charge is dropped because they cannot agree.

● The high priest, Caiaphas, tries a direct question. It is likely that this was breaking the Sanhedrin's own rules. He asks Jesus point blank whether he is the Messiah.

Jesus' reply to the high priest's question shows:

● The Messianic Secret is over. As he is now in the middle of his Passion, he is in truth the Messiah. The Messiah's job is to suffer, die and rise again.

● Jesus will be exalted to the place of honour with God the Father: he will sit at his right hand. (This is picture language, and not to be taken literally.) And he will return. It looks at first as though this will happen soon, because the high priest will see it. But it may mean that he will 'see' or 'realize' that Jesus is at God's right hand: that he is the Son of Man, who will eventually return on the clouds of heaven.

The high priest ceremonially tears his robes, which was a sign that he had heard blasphemy. As the Romans did not allow the council to execute prisoners, he is to be handed over to the governor. Some of them actually assault Jesus, underlining the injustice of the trial and emphasizing that Jesus suffered.

Peter denies Jesus
READ MARK 14 : 66–72

This story must originally have come from Peter. Peter denies Jesus at the same moment as Jesus admits that he is the Messiah. Yet Peter will be forgiven by Jesus (see Mark 16 : 7).

Jesus before Pilate
READ MARK 15 : 1–20

The members of the Sanhedrin meet again in the morning and confirm their plans.

Pontius Pilate was the Roman governor ('procurator' or 'prefect') of Judea. According to the Jewish historian Josephus, he was a cruel and stubborn man.

Jesus is condemned as the Messiah. This is translated as 'king of the Jews' for Pilate's benefit: the crime is treason against Rome. Yet although Jesus is not a political Messiah, it is as the Messiah that he is put to death.

Jesus' reply to Pilate's question ('So you say') means something like, 'You're doing the talking, not me.'

The tradition of Passover amnesty—the release of a prisoner during the festival—is only mentioned by the Gospels. It is odd that Pilate is presented as having to release *either* Barabbas *or* Jesus: why could he not release both? However, it shows that Mark does not think Pilate is really guilty of Jesus' death. The blame lies far more with the people, especially the Jewish authorities. It is important to remember that Christianity spread very quickly through the Roman world. It was bound to attract the attention of the Imperial authorities. They might well not take too kindly to it if they knew its founder had been executed by a Roman judge as a traitor against Rome. So the Gospel writers emphasize that Pilate's hand was forced. He did not really want to execute Jesus.

The crowd chooses a murderer in preference to their Messiah, and Jesus is savagely beaten by being scourged or whipped. The soldiers make fun of his claim to be a king: again, Jesus' suffering is emphasized. He really is a king, even though the soldiers ridicule his claim.

The crucifixion
READ MARK 15 : 21–41

Crucifixion was a form of execution often used by the Romans. It was a savage punishment, designed to cause the maximum suffering and therefore serve as a strong deterrent to others.

The following points about this passage need to be noted:

● Simon of Cyrene helps Jesus to carry the horizontal beam of his cross. Jesus has been beaten too badly to carry it himself. Simon's sons are mentioned, which may show he is an eyewitness, and that his sons are known to Mark's church.

● Golgotha is Aramaic for 'place of the skull'. We are not now certain of the site.

● Jesus refuses the offer of a painkiller (wine mixed with myrrh).

● The execution squad was entitled to a condemned man's clothes, so they dice for them.

● The notice above the cross gave the criminal's offence. Pilate may have meant it to frighten other would-be Messiahs, or as an insult to the Jewish authorities. It underlines, again, that Jesus is executed as the Messiah.

- The fact that Jesus is executed with two bandits shows him in the company of outcasts, even at his death.

- The jeering of the passers-by, and of the chief priests and scribes, misses the point. The Messiah must stay on the cross, not come down from it. This is what his work means.

- The darkness from noon until 3 p.m. may have been a sandstorm or a thunderstorm, or Mark may think it is a supernatural darkness. The Old Testament prophet Amos had predicted that God would make the sun 'go down at noon' (Amos 8 : 9). The darkness shows God is at work.

- *'Eloi, Eloi, lema sabachthani'* is translated: 'My God, my God, why have you abandoned me?' This is a quotation of the first line of Psalm 22. The psalm ends with God saving the person who is suffering. It has been suggested that Jesus has this in mind: God will show him to be in the right, too. However, it is more likely that it underlines the intensity of Jesus' suffering. Even he feels he has been abandoned by God.

- People mistake *Eloi* for 'Elijah', and think he is waiting for the prophet's help. The offer of wine is probably meant as a sick, half-joking experiment.

- When Jesus dies, the Temple curtain is ripped in two. The curtain separated the Holy of Holies, the most sacred part of the Temple, from the rest of the building. This detail may mean one of three things:

  1. The Temple will be destroyed (as it was in AD70 by Rome).

  2. The barrier of sin which separates God and human beings has been destroyed by Jesus' death.

  3. The Temple is no longer the place to find God: God is now to be found in Jesus.

- The centurion confesses Jesus to be the Son of God. It is a Gentile, not a Jew, who makes this statement, and he makes it at the moment of Jesus' death. It is the man on the cross who is most truly the Son of God.

- Some women who had followed Jesus when he was in Galilee watched what happened. Their faithfulness contrasts with the way the male disciples ran away in terror.

Jesus' burial
READ MARK 15 : 42–47

A member of the Sanhedrin, Joseph of Arimathea, asks Pilate for Jesus' body and buries it. Jewish burial customs were strict, and the Romans seem to have respected them here: then, as now, bodies had to be buried on the day of death, if possible. It was made more urgent by the fact that the next day was the Sabbath. The body could not be buried then: that would count as work. The tomb is carefully sealed.

Christians remember the death and burial of Jesus on Good Friday, the Friday of Holy Week.

The resurrection
READ MARK 16 : 1–8

The original text of Mark records the fact of the resurrection, but does not mention any appearances of the risen Jesus to his disciples.

The women go to anoint Jesus' body, which Joseph has not had time to do. The 'young man' is probably meant to be an angel. Jesus is not in the tomb, but has been raised to life. The women are to tell the disciples that Jesus is going before them to Galilee, where they will see him. By singling out Peter for special mention, Mark is probably indicating that Jesus will forgive him.

The women are terrified. This is the sort of fear that the disciples felt when Jesus calmed the storm, and which made the Jews tremble when God gave Moses the Ten Commandments. It is the fear of God: the way people react when God is at work.

The women too are frightened, and say nothing to anyone. Here, the original text of Mark ends.

Christians remember Jesus' resurrection on Easter Day, and on every Sunday. The resurrection has always been at the heart of Christianity. It was and is vitally important:

● It showed that God approved of Jesus.

● It showed that Jesus was who he said he was, and that what he said was true.

● It was God's new saving act. The crucifixion makes no sense without the resurrection. Jesus took away the sins of the world on the cross, and offers people a new life by his resurrection.

● It shows that death is not the end. God raised Jesus to life, and he will raise his people to life as well.

But is it true?

The earliest Christians certainly thought it was. Many of the first disciples died for their faith in Jesus. It is almost impossible to see why they would have died for something they had made up. They were convinced that they had met the risen Jesus. In his first letter to the church at Corinth, Paul says that many of the original eyewitnesses were still alive when he was writing (in AD54/55). He also makes the extraordinary statement that he, too, had seen the risen Jesus. Even non-Christian scholars of the New Testament agree that the disciples genuinely believed that they had experienced the risen Jesus.

It is therefore very difficult to believe that the disciples stole the body or fantasized the whole thing. It is psychologically ridiculous. Neither is it easy to believe that Jesus survived crucifixion and pretended he was risen. That is physically impossible. Furthermore, it makes Jesus a fraud and a liar and the disciples unrealistically stupid. The idea that the disciples hallucinated assumes that they all did so, but hallucinations are seen by individuals, not by groups. And figures in a hallucination do not behave in the way the risen Jesus is said to have behaved. If the Jewish or Roman authorities stole the body, why did they not produce it to kill off the new religion which caused them so much trouble?

Of course, if there is no God, then Jesus remains dead and buried. Yet there are good reasons to believe that there is a God. And these are intelligent, philosophical reasons: they are far more than cultural conditioning. If Jesus was right about God, would not God act in the way that Christians say he did, by raising Jesus from the dead?

The longer ending of Mark
READ MARK 16 : 9–20

This is not part of the original text of Mark. It was added much later by a different author.

Several appearances of the risen Jesus are given:

● Jesus appears to Mary Magdalene. Her companions do not believe her when she tells them about it.

● Jesus appears to two of them while they were walking in the country. Again, the others do not believe it.

● Jesus appears to the eleven disciples while they are at table. They are told to preach the gospel. Those who are baptized and who believe will be saved; the rest will be condemned. Believers will be able to perform miracles.

● Jesus is taken up into heaven. The disciples preached the gospel, which the Lord confirmed by the miracles that accompanied it.

Christians disagree as to whether or not these verses are part of the Bible. The longer ending of Mark looks as though it has been compiled from the other Gospels or similar material. Some of the miracles Jesus says his followers will perform are bizarre, and this, too, casts doubt on the section.

Memory test questions

For examination questions based on Mark, you will need to know the text of the Gospel inside out. These short answer questions are designed to test your knowledge of the text. They follow the order of the Gospel itself.

INTRODUCTION (MARK 1 : 1)

1. In the first verse of Mark, what kind of message describes the book?

2. In the first verse of Mark, which two titles are given to Jesus?

THE PREACHING OF JOHN THE BAPTIST (1 : 2–8)

3. Which prophet predicted John's arrival, according to Mark?

4. In the prophecy, what is the voice (or 'someone') shouting? Where is it shouting?

5. Where did John first appear?

6. People came out to hear John. Where did they come from?

7. In which river did John baptize?

8. What did John wear?

9. What did he eat?

10. John predicted someone would come after him. John said he was not good enough even to—what?

11. When this person arrived, what would he baptize the people with?

JESUS' BAPTISM AND TEMPTATION (1 : 9–13)

12. Jesus came to John to be baptized. From which town did he come?

13. What did Jesus see the heavens do?

14. How did the Holy Spirit descend?

15. What did the voice from heaven say?

16. Where was Jesus tempted?

17. Who made him go there?

18. Who tempted him?

19. How long was he there?

JESUS CALLS THE FIRST DISCIPLES (1 : 14–20)

20. When did Jesus go to preach the Good News in Galilee?

21. What was his message?

22. Where did Jesus meet the first four disciples?

23. The first four disciples were called Simon, Andrew, James and John.
a) Identify the two pairs of brothers.
b) The name of the father of one of the pairs is given. What was his name, and whose father was he?

24. What did they do for a living?

25. What did Jesus say to the first pair he met?

26. When Jesus called his disciples, did they hang around before they followed him?

THE FIRST MIRACLE IN MARK (1 : 21–28)

27. In which building in which town did this miracle take place?

28. What day of the week was it?

29. Why were the people amazed at Jesus' teaching?

30. A man who was possessed by a demon shouted at Jesus. What did he shout?

31. What did Jesus say to the demon?

32. What did the demon do before it left the man?

33. What was the people's reaction?

THE HEALING OF SIMON'S MOTHER-IN-LAW (1 : 29–31)

34. What was wrong with Simon's mother-in-law?

35. How did Jesus heal her?

36. What did she do after she was cured?

THE HEALING OF MANY PEOPLE (1 : 32–34)

37. The people brought to Jesus all the sick and those who were possessed by demons. At what time of day was this?

38. Where did the people gather?

39. Jesus healed the people and drove out the demons. Why did he not allow the demons to say anything?

JESUS PREACHES IN GALILEE (1 : 35–39)

40. Jesus left the house early next morning, before daylight. Where did he go and why?

41. Who found him and what did they say?

42. Jesus said they had to go to the other villages in the area. Why?

43. Where did Jesus preach in Galilee and what did he do?

JESUS HEALS A MAN WITH LEPROSY (1 : 40–45)

44. The leper knelt before Jesus. What did the leper say to him?

45. How does Mark say Jesus felt about this request?

46. How did Jesus cure him?

47. What did Jesus then tell the man to do?

48. How did he disobey Jesus' request?

49. How did this disobedience affect Jesus?

JESUS HEALS A PARALYSED MAN (2 : 1–12)

50. Where did this healing take place?

51. Why were the men bringing the paralysed man not able to get to Jesus?

52. How many men brought the paralysed man?

53. How did they manage to get the paralysed man to Jesus?

54. What did Jesus say to the paralysed man when he saw their faith?

55. Whom did this annoy, and why?

56. How did Jesus prove to them that he had the authority to forgive sins?

57. When Jesus said he had this authority, what did he call himself?

58. The paralysed man picked up his mat and went out. What did the onlookers say?

JESUS CALLS LEVI (2 : 13–17)

59. Where did Jesus return to?

60. Where was Levi when Jesus called him?

61. What did Jesus say to him?

62. What did Levi do?

63. Who was Levi's father?

64. Later on, with whom was Jesus eating?

65. Who asked the disciples, 'Why does he eat with such people?'

66. Jesus' reply said something about a doctor. What?

THE QUESTION ABOUT FASTING (2 : 18–22)

67. Who was fasting, and who was not?

68. Who asked Jesus about this?

69. In Jesus' reply—
a) What will wedding guests not do, and for how long?
b) What will happen to the bridegroom, and what will they then do?
c) What do you not do with a piece of new cloth?

d) What happens if you do?
e) What do you not do with new wine?
f) What happens if you do?
g) What do you use for new wine?

THE SABBATH CORN (2 : 23–28)

70. Where were Jesus and his disciples walking?

71. Who saw them, and what was their complaint?

72. Whom did Jesus refer to in the Old Testament, and what had he done?

73. Complete the following quotation: The _____ was made for the good of _____; _____ was not made for the _____. So the _____ _____ _____ is _____ even of the Sabbath.

JESUS HEALS A MAN WITH A PARALYSED HAND (3 : 1–6)

74. Where did Jesus perform this miracle?

75. 'Some people' were watching Jesus closely. What did they want to see?

76. Jesus called the man out and asked the onlookers, 'What does our Law allow us to do on the Sabbath? To help or to harm? To save a man's life or to destroy it?' What was their reaction, and what did Jesus feel about this?

77. What did he say to the man to heal him?

78. After this incident, which two groups began to plot Jesus' death?

THE HEALING OF MANY PEOPLE (3 : 7–12)

79. Jesus and the disciples went to Lake Galilee (the Sea of Galilee), followed by a crowd. Give **two** places the crowd came from.

80. How did Jesus avoid being crushed by the crowd?

81. Jesus healed people. What did the demons say when they were exorcized, and what did Jesus forbid them to do?

JESUS CALLS THE TWELVE (3 : 13–19)

82. Where did Jesus go to call the Twelve?

83. What did Jesus call the Twelve?

84. What three things were the Twelve to do?

85. Name the Twelve.

86. Who were the Boanerges, and what does the word mean?

JESUS AND BEELZEBUL (3 : 20–30)

87. Jesus went home and a large crowd gathered. They had no time to—what?

88. When his family heard about it, what did they say?

89. Where had the teachers of the Law (scribes) come from?

90. Where did they say Jesus' power to drive out demons came from?

91. Jesus showed their view was silly by speaking of a country and a family. What did he say?

92. If you want to steal a strong man's belongings, what do you have to do first?

93. What is the unforgivable sin, and why did Jesus mention it?

JESUS' MOTHER AND BROTHERS (3 : 31–35)

94. Who did Jesus say were his mother, brother or sister?

THE PARABLE OF THE SOWER AND THE PURPOSE OF THE PARABLES (4 : 1–20)

95. Where did Jesus preach this parable?

96. What happened to the seed that fell along the path?

97. What happened to the seed that fell on rocky ground?

98. What happened to the seed that fell among the thorn bushes?

99. What happened to the seed that fell on good soil?

100. To whom has the secret of the Kingdom of God been given?

101. Who will 'look and look, yet not see' and 'listen and listen, yet not understand'?

102. If those people in question 101 could see and understand, what would happen?

103. In the interpretation of the parable, what does the sower sow?

104. What sort of people are like the seeds that fall along the path?

105. What sort of people are like the seeds that fall on rocky ground?

106. What sort of people are like the seeds that fall among the thorn bushes?

107. What sort of people are like the seeds that produce corn?

MORE PARABLES (4 : 21–34)

108. Where should you not put a lamp?

109. Where should you put it?

110. What will happen to things that are hidden and things that are covered up?

111. What will be the measure you give?

112. What will happen to people who have something?

113. What will happen to people who have nothing?

114. Does the man who plants seed know how it grows?

115. What does the man do when the corn is ripe?

116. How big is a mustard seed?

117. What does it become?

118. What happens in its shade?

119. To whom did Jesus always explain the parables?

JESUS CALMS A STORM (4 : 35–41)

120. What time of day was it when Jesus and the disciples set off for the other side of the Sea of Galilee?

121. What happened to the boat when the strong wind blew up?

122. Where and on what was Jesus sleeping?

123. When the disciples woke him, what did they say?

124. What did Jesus say to the wind?

125. What did he say to the waves?

126. What did he then say to the disciples?

127. Why were the disciples then afraid?

THE MADMAN IN THE TOMBS (5 : 1–20)

128. Where did the boat land?

129. Where did the demoniac live?

130. Why was he no longer chained up?

131. What did he do day and night?

132. He ran to meet Jesus. What did he say at first?

133. What did the man say his name was, and why?

134. What did the spirits beg Jesus?

135. What happened to the pigs, and how many were there?

136. When the news spread around, what did the locals ask Jesus to do?

137. What did the man who was healed want to do?

138. What did Jesus tell him to do instead?

139. Where did the man spread the message about Jesus?

JAIRUS' DAUGHTER AND THE WOMAN WHO TOUCHED JESUS' CLOAK (5 : 21–43)

140. What was Jairus' job?

141. What was wrong with his daughter?

142. What did Jairus ask Jesus to do?

143. What was wrong with the woman who was ill and how long had she suffered from this?

144. Had the doctors been able to help?

145. Why did she want to touch Jesus' clothes?

146. How did Jesus know he had been touched?

147. The woman told Jesus what had happened. What did he say to her?

148. What did the messengers from Jairus' house then say?

149. Who did Jesus take with him to Jairus' house?

150. Jesus said the child was not dead, but—what?

151. Who did Jesus take with him into the room where the girl was, and who did he get to leave?

152. What did Jesus say to raise the child, and what does this mean?

153. When she got up, what did Jesus tell them to do?

154. How old was the child?

JESUS IS REJECTED AT NAZARETH (6 : 1–6)

155. Where and when did Jesus teach in Nazareth?

156. The local people rejected Jesus because they knew him and his family. Name—
a) Jesus' mother
b) Jesus' brothers.

157. What was Jesus' job said to be?

158. Where and by whom does Jesus say a prophet is never respected?

159. What could Jesus not do there?

160. What astonished Jesus?

JESUS SENDS OUT THE TWELVE (6 : 7–13)

161. How many disciples travelled together?

162. Over what did Jesus give them authority?

163. What were they to carry to help them walk?

164. What could they not take?

165. Where should they stay?

166. What sign should they give as a warning to places that do not welcome them?

167. The Twelve cast out demons. How did they heal the sick?

THE DEATH OF JOHN THE BAPTIST (6 : 14–29)

168. Who did Herod think Jesus was?

169. Name Herod's wife.

170. Why had Herod imprisoned John?

171. When was there a celebration for Herod?

172. Who danced?

173. What did Herod promise her?

174. What did her mother tell her to ask for?

175. Why could Herod not refuse?

176. What happened to John's body?

THE FEEDING OF THE FIVE THOUSAND (6 : 30–44)

177. Why did Jesus suggest to the disciples that they should go to a lonely place?

178. People followed them. Why did Jesus have compassion on them?

179. The disciples told Jesus to send the people away to buy food. What did he say to them?

180. What food did the disciples have?

181. How is the grass described?

182. When the people sat down, how big was each group?

183. How many baskets were filled with the leftovers of the meal?

THE WALKING ON THE WATER (6 : 45–52)

184. Where did Jesus send the boat to?

185. What did Jesus do once he had dismissed the crowd?

186. At what time did Jesus walk towards his disciples on the water?

187. What did they think he was?

188. What did Jesus say to reassure them?

189. What happened to the weather when Jesus got into the boat?

190. What could the disciples still not understand?

ANOTHER SUMMARY OF JESUS' HEALINGS (6 : 53–56)

191. Where did they land?

192. What were the sick people lying on?

193. What did they want to touch?

WHAT MAKES A PERSON UNCLEAN? (7 : 1–23)

194. Where had the Pharisees and teachers of the Law (scribes) come from?

195. What had the disciples been doing to break the Law?

196. What were the Pharisees' regulations about ritual washing?

197. Which prophet did Jesus say predicted the Pharisees' hypocrisy?

198. What do the Pharisees put aside, and what do they obey?

199. What is 'Corban', and why did Jesus condemn it?

200. What does Jesus say cannot defile someone (make him or her ritually unclean)?

201. To whom did Jesus have to explain this?

202. Why did he say that things which enter you from outside do not defile you?

203. Mark says Jesus abolished part of the Jewish Law by this. Which part?

204. What does Jesus say defiles a person? Give examples.

JESUS HEALS A GENTILE WOMAN'S DAUGHTER (7 : 24–30)

205. Where did Jesus go for this story?

206. What was wrong with the woman's daughter?

207. Where did the woman come from?

208. Was she a Jew or a Gentile?

209. When she asked Jesus to heal her daughter what did he say about bread and dogs?

210. What did the woman say in reply to this?

211. What did the woman find when she returned home, as Jesus had promised?

JESUS HEALS A DEAF-MUTE (7 : 31–37)

212. Jesus then went towards the Sea of Galilee. What route did he take?

213. How did Jesus heal the man?

214. What did Jesus say, and what does this mean?

215. What did Jesus order the people to do?

216. Did they obey him?

217. Why were the people amazed?

THE FEEDING OF THE FOUR THOUSAND (8 : 1–10)

218. What food did the disciples have?

219. How many baskets of scraps were left over?

THE PHARISEES ASK FOR A SIGN; THE YEAST OF THE PHARISEES AND OF HEROD (8 : 11–21)

220. Did Jesus agree to the Pharisees' request?

221. What had the disciples forgotten?

222. Jesus warned them of the yeast (or leaven) of the Pharisees and of Herod. What did they think he meant?

223. What did Jesus remind them of?

JESUS HEALS A BLIND MAN (8 : 22–26)

224. Where did this healing take place?

225. Where did Jesus take the blind man?

226. What did he do to the man's eyes?

227. What did people look like to him?

228. When he was healed, what did Jesus forbid him to do?

PETER'S DECLARATION ABOUT JESUS (8 : 27—9 : 1)

229. Which town were Jesus and the disciples near?

230. Who did people think Jesus was?

231. Who did Peter say Jesus was?

232. Jesus taught them that the Son of Man must be rejected. By whom?

233. What would happen three days after he is put to death?

234. Who rebuked him for saying this?

235. What did Jesus say to him?

236. Jesus told the crowd that anyone who wants to follow him must—what?

237. What will happen to people who want to save their own lives?

238. What will happen to people who lose their lives for the sake of Jesus and for the gospel?

239. Complete the following:
Does a person gain anything if he wins the
_____ _____ but loses his _____?

240. What will happen to the person who is ashamed of Jesus and his teaching?

241. Some standing there will not taste death until they see—what?

THE TRANSFIGURATION (9 : 2–13)

242. How much later than the above did the Transfiguration take place?

243. Who did Jesus take with him?

244. Where did they go?

245. Jesus' clothes became whiter than—what?

246. Who appeared to Jesus?

247. Who wanted to make what?

248. What overshadowed them?

249. What did the voice from heaven say?

250. When were the disciples allowed to tell what they had seen?

251. Who do the teachers of the Law (scribes) say should come before the Messiah?

252. Had this person in fact come?

JESUS HEALS AN EPILEPTIC BOY (9 : 14–29)

253. Who was arguing with the crowd and the disciples?

254. Who asked Jesus to heal the boy?

255. Who had failed to heal him?

256. What made the boy epileptic?

257. What happened when they brought the boy to Jesus?

258. How long had the condition lasted?

259. For whom is everything possible?

260. When Jesus healed the boy, what did the boy look like at first?

261. The disciples asked Jesus why they could not perform the cure. What drives out this sort of demon?

WHO IS THE GREATEST? (9 : 30–37)

262. What was Jesus teaching his disciples as they went through Galilee?

263. How did they respond to this teaching?

264. What had the disciples been arguing about on the road?

265. What should the person who wants to be first become?

266. If people welcome children in Jesus' name, who do they welcome?

267. If people welcome Jesus, who do they also welcome?

SOME TEACHING OF JESUS (9 : 38–50)

268. Who saw a man driving out demons in Jesus' name?

269. Anyone who is not against Jesus is—what?

270. Who will certainly receive his reward?

271. For whom will it be better to have a millstone tied round his neck and be thrown into the sea?

272. If your right hand causes you to sin, what should you do to it?

273. If your foot causes you to sin, what should you do to it?

274. If your eye causes you to sin, what should you do to it?

275. It is better to enter life maimed than to go—where?

276. What do worms never do?

277. What never happens to the fire?

278. Everything will be purified (or salted) with—what?

279. When is it implied that salt is no good?

280. What should the disciples have in themselves to live in peace with one another?

JESUS' TEACHING ON DIVORCE (10 : 1–12)

281. Who asked Jesus whether the Law allows a man to divorce his wife?

282. What did Moses allow?

283. Why did Jesus say Moses allowed the Jews to do this?

284. Explain why Jesus did not allow divorce.

285. What did Jesus say a man is doing if he divorces his wife and marries again?

286. What did Jesus say a woman is doing if she divorces her husband and marries again?

JESUS BLESSES THE CHILDREN (10 : 13–16)

287. What did Jesus say belongs to the children?

288. What will happen to the person who does not receive the Kingdom of God like a child?

THE RICH MAN (10 : 17–31)

289. What did the rich man ask Jesus?

290. Who did Jesus say was good?

291. What did Jesus tell the man to keep?

292. How long had the man kept these?

293. What did Jesus then tell him to do?

294. What was the rich man's reaction to this?

295. Complete the following:
It is much harder for a _____ person to enter the _____ _____ _____ than for a _____ to go through the _____ of a _____.

296. How did the disciples react to this, and what did they ask each other?

297. What is impossible for God?

298. What did Peter remind Jesus that they had left to follow him?

299. What will such people receive
a) now, and
b) in the age to come,
according to Jesus?

300. What will happen to many who are first, and to many who are last?

JESUS SPEAKS AGAIN ABOUT HIS DEATH (10 : 32–34)

301. Where were Jesus and the disciples heading?

302. Who will condemn the Son of Man to death?

303. To whom will they hand him over?

304. What will they do to the Son of Man when they receive him?

305. What will happen on the third day?

JAMES' AND JOHN'S QUESTION (10 : 35–45)

306. What did James and John ask?

307. What will they drink and be washed with?

308. How did the other disciples react to James' and John's request?

309. Who should the disciples not be like?

310. What should they do to be great?

311. What should they do to be first?

312. What did the Son of Man come to do and to give?

JESUS HEALS BARTIMAEUS (10 : 46–52)

313. What was wrong with Bartimaeus?

314. Where did he live?

315. What did he call Jesus when he shouted out to him?

316. What did Jesus say had made Bartimaeus well?

317. What did he do once he was cured?

THE TRIUMPHAL ENTRY (11 : 1–11)

318. As they approached Jerusalem, they came to a mountain, near two towns. Which mountain and which towns?

319. What did Jesus say the disciples would find in the village?

320. What were they to say if anyone asked them what they were doing?

321. When the disciples brought the animal to Jesus, what did they throw on it?

322. What did people spread on the road?

323. What did the people shout?

324. Where did Jesus go in Jerusalem?

325. As it was late, where did they go then?

THE CURSING OF THE FIG-TREE AND THE CLEANSING OF THE TEMPLE (11 : 12–25)

326. Why were there no figs on the tree?

327. What did Jesus say to the tree?

328. Who did Jesus drive out of the Temple?

329. What did he overturn?

330. What did he prevent them doing in the Temple courtyards?

331. What is the Temple for all the nations?

332. What had they made it?

333. What did the chief priests and teachers of the Law (scribes) do when they heard of this?

334. Why were they afraid of him?

335. What had happened to the fig-tree next morning?

336. What did Jesus say about throwing a hill or a mountain into the sea?

337. If you ask for something in prayer and believe you have received it, what will happen?

338. When you stand and pray, and forgive others, what will God do?

THE QUESTION ABOUT AUTHORITY (11 : 27–33)

339. Who asked Jesus where his authority came from?

340. Where did this take place?

341. What did Jesus ask them in return?

342. Why could they not answer?

343. What answer did they eventually give Jesus?

344. What did Jesus then refuse to tell them?

THE ALLEGORY OF THE VINEYARD (12 : 1–12)

345. What did the man who planted the vineyard dig, and what did he build?

346. What was the owner's slave sent to collect?

347. What did the tenants do to this first servant?

348. What did they do to the next slave?

349. What did they do to the third slave, and to the slaves after that?

350. Who did the owner finally send?

351. Why did the tenants kill this person?

352. What did they do with the body?

353. What will the owner of the vineyard do?

354. What happened to the stone the builders rejected as worthless?

355. Why did the Jewish leaders try to arrest Jesus?

356. Why did they leave him alone?

THE QUESTION ABOUT PAYING TAXES (12 : 13–17)

357. Who asked Jesus about paying taxes?

358. To whom did the taxes go?

359. Whose head was on the denarius (coin)?

360. What should they give to Caesar?

361. What should they give to God?

THE QUESTION ABOUT THE RESURRECTION OF THE DEAD (12 : 18–27)

362. Who asked Jesus about this?

363. What does the Law of Moses say about looking after widows?

364. In their story, how many brothers were there?

365. What did all the brothers do?

366. What was the punchline, which was designed to make belief in the resurrection look silly?

367. What did Jesus say they did not know?

368. When the dead rise to life, what will they be like?

369. What will they then not do?

370. What does God say in the passage about the bush?

371. God is not God of the dead, but—what?

THE GREATEST COMMANDMENT (12 : 28–34)

372. Who asked Jesus about this?

373. Which two commandments did Jesus say were the greatest?

374. The scribe agreed that these two commandments were more important than—what?

375. What did Jesus say the teacher of the Law was not far from?

THE QUESTION ABOUT THE MESSIAH (12 : 35–37)

376. Who asked how the teachers of the Law (scribes) could say the Christ was the Son of David?

377. What did David call the Christ in the psalm?

JESUS WARNS AGAINST THE TEACHERS OF THE LAW (SCRIBES) (12 : 37B–40)

378. What do the teachers of the Law (scribes) like to wear?

379. What do they have in the synagogues?

380. What will they receive?

THE WIDOW'S MITE (12 : 41–44)

381. Where did the widow make her offering?

382. How much did she give?

383. Why, according to Jesus, had she given more than the rich men?

THE END OF THE WORLD (THE APOCALYPTIC DISCOURSE) (13 : 1–37)

Note: *this is not a particularly popular area for examination questions. It is nevertheless worth knowing.*

384. What will happen to the Temple?

385. Where did Jesus deliver his speech about the end of the world?

386. Who will deceive many people?

387. What must happen before the end?

388. When the disciples are arrested and taken to court, who will help them to speak?

389. What will children do to their parents?

390. What will happen to the person who holds out to the end?

391. When they see the 'abomination of desolation' (or 'the awful horror'), what should those in Judea do?

392. What should a man on his roof not do?

393. People should pray to God that the end will not happen—when?

394. Why has God shortened the days of suffering?

395. Who will appear?

396. In the final days, what will happen to the sun and the moon?

397. On what will the Son of Man come?

398. What will the angels do?

399. When the fig-tree puts out its leaves, what does it show?

400. Heaven and earth will pass away. What will not pass away?

401. The Son and the angels do not know when the end will be. Who does?

402. What should the disciples do, since they do not know when the time will come?

403. If the master of the house comes suddenly, what should he not find the disciples doing?

THE PLOT AGAINST JESUS (14 : 1–2)

404. The chief priests and teachers of the Law (scribes) plotted against Jesus. This was two days before a festival. Which one?

405. Why did they not want to arrest Jesus during the festival?

JESUS' ANOINTING (14 : 3–9)

406. In which town was Jesus anointed?

407. Whose house was Jesus eating in?

408. What was the woman's ointment made from?

409. Why were some of the people angry?

410. What did Jesus say about the poor?

411. Why did Jesus say the woman had anointed his body?

JUDAS (14 : 10–11)

412. What did the Jewish leaders agree to give Judas?

THE LAST SUPPER (14 : 12–31)

413. Who would show the disciples the place for them to eat the Passover meal with Jesus?

414. Which day of the festival was this, and what did the Jews do then?

415. One of the Twelve would dip his bread in the dish with Jesus. Which one would that be?

416. What did Jesus say the bread was?

417. What did Jesus say the wine was?

418. What did Jesus' blood seal?

419. When would Jesus next drink wine?

420. After they had sung a hymn, where did they go?

421. What did Jesus predict the disciples would all do?

422. Which disciple said he would not?

423. When Jesus was raised to life, where would he go before the disciples to?

424. What would happen before the cock crowed twice?

JESUS IN GETHSEMANE (14 : 32–52)

425. Who did Jesus take with him?

426. What did Jesus call God in his prayer?

427. What did he ask God to do?

428. What were the disciples doing while he was praying?

429. How many times did he find them like this?

430. With whom did Judas arrive?

431. What was the sign Judas would give to identify Jesus to the crowd?

432. Who attacked whom?

433. Who ran away naked?

JESUS' TRIAL BEFORE THE SANHEDRIN (14 : 53–65)

434. Where did Peter go?

435. Did the witnesses against Jesus agree?

436. What was the accusation against Jesus about the Temple?

437. The High Priest asked Jesus if he had any answer to the accusations brought against him. What did Jesus say in reply?

438. The High Priest then asked Jesus, 'Are you the Messiah, the Son of the Blessed God?' What was Jesus' reply?

439. What did the High Priest tear?

440. Of what crime was Jesus found guilty?

441. How did they mock Jesus?

PETER DENIES JESUS (14 : 66–72)

442. Who first recognized Peter?

443. What happened immediately after Peter first said he did not know Jesus?

444. What made the bystanders sure that Peter was a disciple?

445. What did Peter do when the cock crowed a second time?

JESUS BEFORE PILATE (15 : 1–20)

446. Give Pilate's first name.

447. Before they handed Jesus over to Pilate, what did the Sanhedrin do first thing in the morning?

448. What was the first question Pilate asked Jesus?

449. What was Jesus' reply?

450. The chief priests accused Jesus of many things. Pilate asked him if he was going to answer them. What did Jesus say?

451. Who was Barabbas?

452. The governor used to set free one prisoner as a special favour. At what time of year did he do this?

453. What did Pilate ask the crowd?

454. Who did the crowd ask for?

455. Why did they ask for him?

456. What did they want done with Jesus?

457. Why did Pilate give in to them?

458. What happened to Jesus before he was handed over for crucifixion?

459. How did Pilate's soldiers mock Jesus?

THE CRUCIFIXION (15 : 21–41)

460. Who was Simon of Cyrene?

461. Name the place where Jesus was crucified, and give its meaning.

462. What was Jesus offered as a painkiller?

463. Did he take it?

464. What did the soldiers do about Jesus' clothes?

465. What time was it when Jesus was crucified?

466. Give the wording of the notice above Jesus' head.

467. Who was crucified with Jesus?

468. What were the insults of
a) the passers-by?
b) the chief priests and the teachers of the Law (scribes)?

469. When did the darkness start to cover the land, and how long did it last?

470. What did Jesus cry, and what does it mean?

471. Who did the people think he was calling?

472. What was Jesus offered on a sponge?

473. Why was he offered this?

474. Jesus died. What happened in the Temple?

475. When the centurion saw how Jesus died, what did he say?

476. Who was looking on from a distance?

JESUS' BURIAL (15 : 42–47)

477. Who provided Jesus' tomb?

478. What was he looking for or waiting for?

479. What was he a member of?

480. When did he ask Pilate for Jesus' body?

481. Why was Pilate surprised?

482. Who saw where Jesus was laid?

THE RESURRECTION (16 : 1–8)

483. Why did the women go to the tomb?

484. When did they go there?

485. What was worrying them on the way?

486. Who did they meet in the tomb?

487. What was the message to the disciples and to Peter?

488. Why did the women keep silent about this?

THE LONGER ENDING OF MARK (16 : 9–20)

Note: *this was not written by the author of Mark. It was added later. Most translations print it after Mark 16 : 8, but it is not part of the Gospel.*

489. To whom did the risen Jesus first appear?

490. To whom did Jesus appear while they walked to the country?

491. When did Jesus appear to the eleven, and why did he scold them?

492. What did he tell them to do?

493. What happened after Jesus had talked with them?

PART 5

Memory test answers

Note: when quotations are used, they are taken from the Good News Bible. Other translations may be slightly different.

INTRODUCTION (1 : 1)

1. Good News or Gospel.
2. Christ, Son of God.

THE PREACHING OF JOHN THE BAPTIST (1 : 2–8)

3. Isaiah.
4. The voice shouts an instruction to prepare the way for the Lord and to make his path straight. The voice is said to be shouting in the desert.
5. In the desert.
6. Judea and Jerusalem.
7. The Jordan.
8. Clothes made from camel's hair and a leather belt.
9. Locusts and wild honey.
10. Undo his sandal strap.
11. The Holy Spirit.

JESUS' BAPTISM AND TEMPTATION (1 : 9–13)

12. Nazareth.
13. Open.
14. 'Like a dove.'
15. 'You are my own dear Son. I am pleased with you.'
16. The desert.
17. The Spirit.
18. Satan.
19. Forty days.

JESUS CALLS THE FIRST DISCIPLES (1 : 14–20)

20. After John had been arrested.
21. 'The right time has come and the Kingdom of God is near! Turn away from your sins and believe the Good News!'
22. By the Sea of Galilee.
23. a) Simon was Andrew's brother; James was John's brother.
    b) Zebedee. He was James and John's father.
24. They were fishermen.

25. 'Come with me, and I will teach you to catch men.'
26. No, they followed him straight away!

THE FIRST MIRACLE IN MARK (1 : 21–28)

27. In the synagogue in Capernaum.
28. The Sabbath.
29. They were amazed because he taught them 'with authority', unlike the teachers of the Law (scribes).
30. 'What do you want with us, Jesus of Nazareth? Are you here to destroy us? I know who you are— you are God's holy messenger!'
31. 'Be quiet, and come out of the man.'
32. It shook him hard and screamed.
33. They were amazed at Jesus' new teaching and at his power over the demons, and the news about him spread over Galilee.

THE HEALING OF SIMON'S MOTHER-IN-LAW (1 : 29–31)

34. She had a fever.
35. He took her by the hand and helped her up.
36. She waited on them.

THE HEALING OF MANY PEOPLE (1 : 32–34)

37. That evening after sunset.
38. In front of the house.
39. Because they knew who he was.

JESUS PREACHES IN GALILEE (1 : 35–39)

40. He went to a lonely place to pray.
41. Simon and his companions found him and said, 'Everyone is looking for you.'
42. He had to preach to them because that was why he came.
43. He preached in the synagogues and drove out demons.

JESUS HEALS A MAN WITH LEPROSY (1 : 40–45)

44. 'If you want to, you can make me clean.'
45. He was filled with pity or he was angry. (The manuscripts of Mark give either.)
46. He touched him and said, 'Be clean!'

47. He told the man not to tell anyone, but to go to the priest and offer the sacrifice which Moses commanded as a proof to the people.

48. He spread the news everywhere.

49. He was unable to go into a town publicly, and had to stay in lonely places, where people came to him.

JESUS HEALS A PARALYSED MAN (2 : 1–12)

50. In Capernaum.

51. Because a crowd had gathered outside the house.

52. Four.

53. They made a hole in the roof and lowered the paralysed man down on his mat.

54. 'My son, your sins are forgiven.'

55. It annoyed the teachers of the Law (scribes). It was blasphemy: only God could forgive sins.

56. He said to the paralysed man, 'I tell you, pick up your mat and go home!'

57. The Son of Man.

58. 'We have never seen anything like this!'

JESUS CALLS LEVI (2 : 13–17)

59. The shore of the Sea (or Lake) of Galilee.

60. In his office.

61. 'Follow me.'

62. He got up and followed him.

63. Alphaeus.

64. Levi, other tax collectors and sinners (or outcasts) and the disciples.

65. Some teachers of the Law (scribes), who were Pharisees.

66. 'People who are well do not need a doctor, but only those who are sick. I have not come to call respectable people, but outcasts.'

THE QUESTION ABOUT FASTING (2 : 18–22)

67. The disciples of John the Baptist and the Pharisees were fasting; Jesus and his disciples were not.

68. 'Some people.' (Not specified.)

69. a) Fast as long as the bridegroom is with them.
b) The bridegroom will be taken away from them and then they will fast.
c) Patch an old coat or garment.
d) The patch will shrink and make an even bigger hole.
e) Put it in old wineskins.
f) The wine will burst the skins and both will be ruined.
g) Fresh wineskins.

THE SABBATH CORN (2 : 23–28)

70. Through some cornfields.

71. The Pharisees. They complained that Jesus and his disciples were breaking the Law (Torah), since it was a Sabbath.

72. David. He and his men were hungry, so David went to the house of God and ate the ceremonial bread. He also gave some to his men. The Torah said only the priests could eat this bread.

73. The Sabbath was made for the good of man; man was not made for the Sabbath. So the Son of Man is Lord even of the Sabbath.

JESUS HEALS A MAN WITH A PARALYSED HAND (3 : 1–6)

74. In the synagogue.

75. Whether Jesus would heal on the Sabbath.

76. They were silent. Jesus was angry and grieved at their stubbornness.

77. 'Stretch out your hand.'

78. The Pharisees and the Herodians (members of Herod's party).

THE HEALING OF MANY PEOPLE (3 : 7–12)

79. Any two from—
Galilee
Judea
Jerusalem
Idumea
the East of the Jordan
area around Tyre and Sidon

80. He got into a boat.

81. The demons said, 'You are the Son of God!' Jesus ordered them not to tell anyone who he was.

JESUS CALLS THE TWELVE (3 : 13–19)

82. Up a hill.

83. Apostles.

84. To be with Jesus, to preach and to cast out demons.

85. Simon Peter
James)
John) sons of Zebedee
Andrew
Philip
Bartholomew
Matthew
Thomas
James son of Alphaeus
Thaddaeus
Simon the Zealot (or Patriot)
Judas Iscariot

86. James and John. It means 'sons (or men) of thunder'.

JESUS AND BEELZEBUL (3 : 20–30)

87. Eat.

88. 'He is beside himself' or 'He's gone mad!'

89. Jerusalem.

90. From Beelzebul.

91. If a country or a family divide themselves into groups, they will fall apart. So if Satan's kingdom divides itself into groups, it is coming to an end.

92. Tie up the strong man.

93. Blasphemy against the Holy Spirit. Jesus mentioned it because they were saying he was possessed by a demon.

JESUS' MOTHER AND BROTHERS (3 : 31–35)

94. Whoever does the will of God.

THE PARABLE OF THE SOWER AND THE PURPOSE OF THE PARABLES (4 : 1–20)

95. Jesus was sitting in a boat near the shore of the Sea of Galilee.

96. Birds ate it.

97. It sprouted quickly because the soil was not deep, but it was scorched by the sun.

98. The thorn bushes choked the plants.

99. It grew up and produced thirty grains, sixty grains or a hundred grains.

100. The Twelve and some of those with them.

101. 'Those outside', who have not been given the secret of the Kingdom.

102. They would turn to God and be forgiven.

103. The word (God's message).

104. Those who hear the message and immediately it is taken away by Satan.

105. Those who hear the word gladly, but it does not sink in. When persecution comes, they give up.

106. Those in whom the message does not bear fruit because they are so wrapped up in the world.

107. Those who accept the message and bear fruit.

MORE PARABLES (4 : 21–34)

108. Under a bowl or a bed.

109. On a lampstand.

110. Hidden things will be brought into the open; things covered up will be uncovered.

111. The measure you receive. (The Good News Bible takes this to mean that the rules you use to judge others will be used by God to judge you.)

112. They will be given more.

113. Even what they have will be taken away.

114. No.

115. Harvests it with his sickle.

116. It is the smallest seed in the world.

117. The biggest of all plants.

118. Birds make their nests.

119. To the disciples.

JESUS CALMS A STORM (4 : 35–41)

120. Evening.

121. Waves began to fill the boat.

122. In the stern: his head was on a pillow.

123. 'Teacher, don't you care that we are about to die?'

124. 'Be quiet!'

125. 'Be still!'

126. 'Why are you frightened? Have you still no faith?'

127. Because they wondered who Jesus was, when the wind and waves obeyed him.

THE MADMAN IN THE TOMBS (5 : 1–20)

128. In the territory of Gerasa or Gadara.

129. Among the tombs.

130. Because he kept smashing the chains.

131. Scream and cut himself with stones.

132. 'Jesus, Son of the Most High God! What do you want with me? For God's sake, I beg you, don't punish me!'

133. Legion (or Mob) because there were so many of them.

134. To let them go into the pigs.

135. They rushed into the Lake and were drowned. About 2,000.

136. Leave their territory.

137. Go with Jesus.

138. 'Go back home to your family and tell them how much the Lord has done for you and how kind he has been to you.'

139. Throughout the Decapolis (Ten Towns).

JAIRUS' DAUGHTER AND THE WOMAN WHO TOUCHED JESUS' CLOAK (5 : 21–43)

140. Ruler (or official) of the synagogue.

141. She was 'very ill'.

142. Come and lay his hands on her.

143. She had had a severe bleeding for twelve years.

144. No: in fact, she got worse.

145. She thought, 'If I just touch his clothes, I will get well.'

146. He felt the power go forth from him.

147. 'My daughter, your faith has made you well. Go in peace, and be healed of your trouble.'

148. Jairus' daughter was dead: there was no point in troubling Jesus further.

149. Peter, James and John.

150. Sleeping.

151. He took with him Peter, James, John and the girl's parents, and got the mourners or bystanders to leave.

152. 'Talitha koum.' 'Little girl, I tell you to get up.'

153. Give her something to eat.

154. Twelve.

JESUS IS REJECTED AT NAZARETH (6 : 1–6)

155. In the synagogue on the Sabbath.

156. a) Mary.
    b) James, Joseph, Judas, Simon.

157. Carpenter.

158. In his home town, by his relatives and family.

159. Miracles, although he healed a few sick people.

160. Their lack of faith.

JESUS SENDS OUT THE TWELVE (6 : 7–13)

161. Two.

162. Evil spirits.

163. A stick.

164. Bread, a beggar's bag, money, an extra shirt.

165. In one house until they leave the area.

166. Shake the dust from their feet.

167. They anointed them with oil.

THE DEATH OF JOHN THE BAPTIST (6 : 14–29)

168. John the Baptist, raised from the dead.

169. Herodias.

170. Because Herodias wanted him to: John had condemned their marriage, since she was already married to Philip, Herod's brother.

171. On his birthday.

172. Herodias' daughter. Her name was Salome, but this is not mentioned by Mark.

173. Anything she wanted, up to half his kingdom.

174. John the Baptist's head on a dish.

175. Because he had made a vow in front of his guests to give the girl what she asked for.

176. His disciples buried it.

THE FEEDING OF THE FIVE THOUSAND (6 : 30–44)

177. So they could rest: there were so many people coming and going that they did not even have time to eat.

178. Because they were like sheep without a shepherd.

179. 'You yourselves give them something to eat.'

180. Five loaves, two fish.

181. It was green.

182. Some groups numbered a hundred, others numbered fifty.

183. Twelve.

THE WALKING ON THE WATER (6 : 45–52)

184. Bethsaida.

185. He went up a hill to pray.

186. Between 3 and 6 a.m. (about the fourth watch).

187. A ghost.

188. 'Courage! It is I. Don't be afraid.'

189. The wind died down.

190. About the loaves (the meaning of the feeding miracle).

ANOTHER SUMMARY OF JESUS' HEALINGS (6 : 53–56)

191. Gennesaret.

192. Mats.

193. The edge of his cloak.

WHAT MAKES A PERSON UNCLEAN? (1 : 1–23)

194. Jerusalem.

195. Eating with unwashed hands.

196. To wash hands ritually before eating;
    to eat nothing from the market without first washing it;
    or wash themselves after coming from the market before eating (the Greek can mean either);
    to wash cups, pots, copper bowls and beds ritually.

197. Isaiah.

198. They put aside God's commands and obey men's teaching.

199. 'Corban' means 'devoted to God'. Property or wealth could be declared corban. Some people used it to get round the commandment to honour their father and mother. This is why Jesus condemned it.

200. What goes into a person from outside.

201. The disciples.

202. Because they do not enter the heart but the stomach, and then pass on.

203. The food regulations.

204. A person is defiled by what comes out of him: evil ideas, greed, fornication (not in the Good News Bible translation), theft, evil things, murder, deceit, adultery, indecency, jealousy, slander, pride, folly.

JESUS HEALS A GENTILE WOMAN'S DAUGHTER (7 : 24–30)

205. To a house near Tyre.

206. She was possessed by a demon.

207. From Phoenicia in Syria.

208. Gentile.

209. 'Let us first feed the children. It isn't right to take the children's food and throw it to the dogs.'

210. 'Sir, even the dogs under the table eat the children's leftovers.'

211. The demon had gone out of her daughter.

JESUS HEALS A DEAF-MUTE (7 : 31–37)

212. He went from near Tyre to Sidon, and then through the Ten Towns (Decapolis).

213. He took him away from the crowd, put his fingers in his ears, spat and touched the man's tongue.

214. 'Ephphatha.' 'Open up!'

215. Not to talk about it to anyone.

216. No.

217. Because Jesus did everything well, even making the deaf hear and the dumb speak.

THE FEEDING OF THE FOUR THOUSAND (8 : 1–10)

218. Seven loaves; a few fish.

219. Seven baskets.

THE PHARISEES ASK FOR A SIGN; THE YEAST OF THE PHARISEES AND OF HEROD (8 : 11–21)

220. No.

221. To bring enough bread.

222. They thought he was talking about their forgetting to bring enough bread.

223. The number of baskets of leftovers after the two feeding miracles.

JESUS HEALS A BLIND MAN (8 : 22–26)

224. Bethsaida.

225. Out of the village.

226. He spat on them and placed his hands on them.

227. Trees, but they walk around!

228. Enter the village.

PETER'S DECLARATION ABOUT JESUS (8 : 27—9 : 1)

229. Caesarea Philippi.

230. John the Baptist, Elijah, one of the prophets.

231. The Christ (Messiah).

232. The elders, the chief priests, the teachers of the Law (scribes).

233. He will rise.

234. Peter.

235. 'Get away from me, Satan. Your thoughts don't come from God but from man!'

236. Forget self and carry his cross.

237. They will lose them.

238. They will save them.

239. Does a person gain anything if he wins the whole world but loses his life?

240. The Son of Man will be ashamed of him when he comes in the glory of the Father with the holy angels.

241. The Kingdom of God come with power.

THE TRANSFIGURATION (9 : 2–13)

242. Six days.

243. Peter, James and John.

244. Up a mountain.

245. Anything on earth could bleach them.

246. Elijah and Moses.

247. Peter wanted to make three tents.

248. A cloud.

249. 'This is my own dear Son—listen to him!'

250. When the Son of Man had risen from death.

251. Elijah.

252. Yes, but (it is implied) as John the Baptist.

JESUS HEALS AN EPILEPTIC BOY (9 : 14–29)

253. Teachers of the Law (scribes)

254. His father.

255. The disciples.

256. A demon.

257. The demon threw the boy into a fit.

258. From his childhood.

259. For one who has faith.

260. A dead body.

261. Prayer.

WHO IS THE GREATEST? (9 : 30–37)

262. That the Son of Man would suffer and rise again.

263. They did not understand and were afraid to ask.

264. Who was the greatest.

265. Last and servant of all.

266. Jesus.

267. The one who sent Jesus: God.

SOME TEACHING OF JESUS (9 : 38–50)

268. John.

269. For him.

270. Anyone who gives a disciple a cup of water because they bear Christ's name.

271. Anyone who causes one of 'these little ones' to sin (or to lose their faith).

272. Cut it off.

273. Cut it off.

274. Pluck it out.

275. To hell.

276. Die.

277. It is never put out.

278. Fire.

279. When it has lost its saltiness.

280. Salt. (The Good News Bible has 'salt of friendship'.)

JESUS' TEACHING ON DIVORCE (10 : 1–12)

281. Some Pharisees.

282. Moses allowed a man to give his wife a divorce note and send her away.

283. Because of their hardness of heart (or because they were so hard to teach).

284. Because in the beginning, God made humans male and female. In Genesis, it says, 'for this reason a man will leave his father and mother and unite with his wife, and the two will become one.' They are no longer two, but one. What God has joined, no one must separate.

285. Committing adultery against his wife.

286. Committing adultery against her husband.

JESUS BLESSES THE CHILDREN (10 : 13–16)

287. The Kingdom of God.

288. He shall never enter it.

THE RICH MAN (10 : 17–31)

289. 'Good Teacher, what must I do to receive eternal life?'

290. No one, except God.

291. The commandments.

292. Since he was young.

293. Sell everything, give the money to the poor and follow Jesus.

294. He went away, sad.

295. It is much harder for a rich person to enter the Kingdom of God than for a camel to go through the eye of a needle.

296. They were astonished and asked, 'Who, then, can be saved?'

297. Nothing.

298. Everything.

299. a) A hundred times more houses, brothers, sisters, mothers, children, fields and persecutions.
b) eternal life.

300. Many who are first will be last; many who are last will be first.

JESUS SPEAKS AGAIN ABOUT HIS DEATH (10 : 32–34)

301. Jerusalem.

302. The chief priests and the teachers of the Law (scribes).

303. To the Gentiles.

304. Mock him, spit on him, whip him and kill him.

305. He will rise to life.

JAMES AND JOHN'S QUESTION (10 : 35–45)

306. To sit on Jesus' right and left hand in the Kingdom.

307. They will drink the cup which Jesus will drink and be washed with the baptism with which Jesus will be washed.

308. They were angry with them.

309. The rulers of the Gentiles.

310. Become the others' servant.

311. Become the slave of all.

312. Not to be served but to serve, and to give his life to redeem many.

JESUS HEALS BARTIMAEUS (10 : 46–52)

313. He was blind.

314. Jericho.

315. 'Jesus, Son of David!'

316. His faith.

317. Followed him on the road.

THE TRIUMPHAL ENTRY (11 : 1–11)

318. The Mount of Olives. Bethphage and Bethany.

319. A colt tied up, which had never been ridden.

320. The master needs it, and will send it back at once.

321. Their cloaks.

322. Their cloaks or branches.

323. 'Praise God!' (or 'Hosanna!') 'God bless him who comes in the name of the Lord! God bless the coming Kingdom of King David, our father! Praise God!' (or 'Hosanna!')

324. To the Temple.

325. To Bethany.

THE CURSING OF THE FIG-TREE AND THE CLEANSING OF THE TEMPLE (11 : 12–25)

326. Because it was the wrong time of year.

327. 'No one shall ever eat figs from you again!'

328. Those who were buying and selling.

329. The money-changers' tables and the stools of the pigeon-sellers.

330. Carrying anything through.

331. A house of prayer.

332. A hideout for thieves.

333. They began to look for a way to kill Jesus.

334. Because the crowd were amazed by his teaching.

335. It had withered.

336. 'I assure you that whoever tells this hill to get up and throw itself in the sea and does not doubt in his heart, but believes that what he says will happen, it will be done for him.'

337. You will be given what you ask for.

338. Forgive you.

THE QUESTION ABOUT AUTHORITY (11 : 27–33)

339. The chief priests, the teachers of the Law (scribes) and the elders.

340. In the Temple.

341. Where did John get his authority to baptize from?

342. Because if they said, 'from God', Jesus would ask why they did not believe him. They could not say, 'from men', because they were afraid of the crowd.

343. 'We don't know.'

344. Where his authority came from.

THE ALLEGORY OF THE VINEYARD (12 : 1–12)

345. He dug a hole for the winepress, and he built a watchtower.

346. His share of the harvest.

347. Beat him and sent him away empty-handed.

348. Beat him over the head and 'treated him shamefully'.

349. They killed the third slave, and beat and killed the others.

350. His own dear son.

351. So the inheritance would pass to them.

352. Threw it out of the vineyard.

353. Kill the tenants and give the vineyard to others.

354. It became the head of the corner or the most important stone of all.

355. Because they knew he had told the parable against them.

356. Because they were afraid of the crowd.

THE QUESTION ABOUT PAYING TAXES (12 : 13–17)

357. Some Pharisees and Herodians (members of Herod's party).

358. To Rome (to Caesar).

359. Caesar's.

360. The things that are Caesar's.

361. The things that are God's.

THE QUESTION ABOUT THE RESURRECTION OF THE DEAD (12 : 18–27)

362. The Sadducees.

363. If a man dies, leaving a childless wife, his brother must marry the widow. They can then have children who will be considered the dead man's children.

364. Seven.

365. Marry the widow of the eldest brother.

366. Whose wife would the widow be at the resurrection?

367. The scriptures and the power of God.

368. The angels in heaven.

369. Marry.

370. 'I am the God of Abraham, the God of Isaac, and the God of Jacob.'

371. God of the living.

THE GREATEST COMMANDMENT (12 : 28–34)

372. A scribe (teacher of the Law).

373. (i) Listen, Israel! The Lord our God is the only Lord. Love the Lord your God with all your heart, with all your soul, with all your mind, and with all your strength.
(ii) Love your neighbour as you love yourself.

374. Animal sacrifices and other sacrifices.

375. The Kingdom of God.

THE QUESTION ABOUT THE MESSIAH (12 : 35–37)

376. Jesus.

377. Lord.

JESUS WARNS AGAINST THE TEACHERS OF THE LAW (SCRIBES) (12 : 37B–40)

378. Long robes.

379. The best seats.

380. The worse punishment.

THE WIDOW'S MITE (12 : 41–44)

381. In the Temple treasury.

382. Two copper coins, worth a penny.

383. Because she gave all she had to live on.

THE END OF THE WORLD (THE APOCALYPTIC DISCOURSE) (13 : 1–37)

384. Not one stone will be left in its place.

385. On the Mount of Olives.

386. Many who will say, 'I am he!' They will claim to speak for Jesus.

387. The gospel must be preached to all peoples.

388. The Holy Spirit.

389. Turn against them and have them put to death.

390. He will be saved.

391. Flee to the hills.

392. Go down to the house to get something to take with him.

393. In winter.

394. For the sake of his chosen people.

395. False Christs and false prophets.

396. The sun will grow dark; the moon will no longer shine.

397. Clouds.

398. Gather God's chosen people from one end of the world to the other.

399. That summer is near.

400. Jesus' words.

401. The Father.

402. Watch (or keep awake).

403. Sleeping.

THE PLOT AGAINST JESUS (14 : 1–2)

404. The Festival of Passover and Unleavened Bread.

405. Because the people might riot.

JESUS' ANOINTING (14 : 3–9)

406. Bethany.

407. Simon the leper's house. (Or the house of Simon who had a dreaded skin disease).

408. Pure nard.

409. Because the ointment could have been sold, and the money given to the poor.

410. 'You will always have poor people with you, and any time you want to, you can help them.'

411. For burial.

JUDAS (14 : 10–11)

412. Money. (It is not said how much.)

THE LAST SUPPER (14 : 12–31)

413. A man carrying a water jar in the city.

414. The first day of the Festival of Unleavened Bread. The Passover lambs were killed.

415. The one who would betray him.

416. His body.

417. His blood.

418. God's covenant.

419. In the Kingdom of God.

420. To the Mount of Olives.

421. Run away.

422. Peter.

423. Galilee.

424. Peter would deny Jesus three times.

JESUS IN GETHSEMANE (14 : 32–52)

425. Peter, James and John.

426. Abba ('My Father').

427. Take the cup of suffering away from him.

428. Sleeping.

429. Three.

430. An armed crowd, sent by the Jewish authorities.

431. He would kiss him.

432. 'One of those standing there' (Mark does not identify him) cut off the ear of the high priest's slave.

433. A young man.

JESUS' TRIAL BEFORE THE SANHEDRIN (14 : 53–65)

434. To the high priest's courtyard.

435. No.

436. That he would destroy the Temple and build another after three days, that was not built with hands.

437. Nothing.

438. 'I am, and you will all see the Son of Man seated on the right of the Almighty' (or 'Power') 'and coming with the clouds of heaven.'

439. His robe.

440. Blasphemy.

441. He was spat on, blindfolded and beaten. While he was blindfolded, they said, 'Guess who hit you!' (or 'Prophesy!')

PETER DENIES JESUS (14 : 66–72)

442. A servant girl.

443. A cock crowed. (According to most Greek copies of Mark. Some leave this detail out.)

444. He was from Galilee.

445. He wept.

JESUS BEFORE PILATE (15 : 1–20)

446. Pontius.

447. They held another meeting.

448. 'Are you the king of the Jews?'

449. 'So you say.'

450. Nothing.

451. A prisoner who had committed murder during a riot.

452. At Passover.

453. 'Do you want me to set free for you the King of the Jews?'

454. Barabbas.

455. Because the chief priests had stirred them up to ask for him.

456. They wanted him crucified.

457. He wanted to please them.

458. He was whipped.

459. They put a purple robe on him, and made a crown of thorns. They saluted him, saying, 'Long live the King of the Jews!', beat him, spat on him and bowed to him in homage.

THE CRUCIFIXION (15 : 21–41)

460. The man who carried Jesus' cross.

461. Golgotha. 'Place of the Skull.'

462. Wine mixed with myrrh.

463. No.

464. They diced for them.

465. 9 a.m. (The third hour).

466. The King of the Jews.

467. Two robbers.

468. a) Aha! You were going to tear down the Temple and build it up again in three days! Now come down from the cross and save yourself!
b) He saved others, but he cannot save himself! Let us see the Messiah, the King of Israel, come down from the cross now, and we will believe in him!

469. Noon (the sixth hour). Three hours.

470. 'Eloi, Eloi, lema sabachthani?' 'My God, my God, why did you abandon me?'

471. Elijah.

472. Cheap wine (vinegar).

473. Because the bystanders wanted to see whether Elijah would come to take him down.

474. The curtain was torn in two, from top to bottom.

475. 'This man was really the Son of God!'

476. The women: Mary Magdalene, Mary the mother of the younger James and of Joseph and Salome.

JESUS' BURIAL (15 : 42–47)

477. Joseph of Arimathea.

478. The Kingdom of God.

479. The Sanhedrin.

480. The day of Preparation. (The day before the Sabbath.)

481. Because Jesus was already dead.

482. Mary Magdalene and Mary the mother of Joseph.

THE RESURRECTION (16 : 1–8)

483. To anoint Jesus' body.

484. At sunrise on Sunday morning.

485. Who was going to roll back the stone from the tomb's entrance.

486. A young man, dressed in white.

487. 'He is going to Galilee ahead of you; there you will see him, just as he told you.'

488. Because they were frightened.

THE LONGER ENDING OF MARK (16 : 9–20)

489. Mary Magdalene.

490. To two of them.

491. He appeared to the eleven at table and scolded them because they had not believed he was risen.

492. Preach the gospel to everyone.

493. He was taken up into heaven and sat at God's right hand.

Practice GCSE questions

These practice exam questions are based closely on the sort of questions which have actually been set in GCSE papers. Practising answering them should form an important part of your revision. Once you feel confident in this, you should try doing some of them as timed exercises. Decide which one you are going to try, then give yourself as much time to answer it as you will have in the examination. In this way you will improve your exam technique—and by checking your answers you will improve your knowledge as well.

Notice that each question is divided into a number of parts which test different things. There are **knowledge** questions, **understanding** questions and **evaluation** questions. The evaluation questions ask you to give your opinion about various things. Candidates often find evaluation questions difficult and lose marks by writing down the first thing which comes into their heads—often simple gut reactions. It is important that you do not fall into the same trap.

Look at Question 1 below. The evaluation question is section (d).

Remember when answering evaluation questions that you are sitting a **Religious Studies** examination. Don't waffle! Base your answer on religious principles and use the opportunity to show off your knowledge of Mark's Gospel. You can do this by backing up your opinions with suitable quotations from the Gospel that you have not used elsewhere.

Have a go at Question 1 now, then go on to choose some others to do according to your revision plan. (The figures in brackets at the end of the questions give the number of marks available.)

1.   (a) Mark says that Jesus was often accompanied by his disciples.
      (i)   Who does Mark say were his first two disciples? (1)
      (ii) What was their occupation before being called by Jesus? (1)
      (iii) Explain why Jesus might have chosen people like these. (4)

(b) Describe another occasion in Mark's Gospel when Jesus asks somebody to become his disciple. (4)

(c) On one occasion, Jesus sent out twelve of his closest followers.
      (i)   Name TWO of the things he told them to do. (2)
      (ii) What can tell us about the way Jesus expected his followers to live? (4)

(d) 'Jesus asked too much of his disciples. Living up to his expectations would be impossible.' How would you reply to somebody who said this? Give your reasons. (4)

2.   (a) Jesus invited Levi to become his disciple.
      (i)   What was Levi's occupation? (1)
      (ii) Explain why people were shocked when Jesus took a meal at Levi's house. (3)
      (iii) What did Jesus say to them? (4)

(b) Explain why Jesus' actions in this story particularly offended the Pharisees. (4)

(c) Describe how people today might follow the example of
      (i)   Jesus AND
      (ii) Levi. (4)

(d) In your opinion, are there any particular difficulties with living the life of a disciple of Jesus today, and can these be overcome? Explain your answer. (4)

3. Mark begins his Gospel with an account of the teaching of John the Baptist.

(a) According to Mark, what was John preparing people for, and how did he do this? (4)

(b) What did John say about himself and the man who was to come after him? (4)

(c) Describe what happened at Jesus' baptism. (4)

(d) Why do you think that people were so eager to hear John and be baptized by him? (4)

(e) 'I can believe in God, but the idea that Jesus was his Son is just too far-fetched. Why should he bother to send his Son?' How would you respond to views like these? Give reasons for your answer. (4)

4. (a) At the beginning of his Gospel, Mark makes it clear that John the Baptist was like the prophet Elijah. Explain both HOW and WHY he does this. (4)

(b) (i) What were the words Jesus heard at his baptism? (2)
    (ii) Explain their meaning (4)

(c) 'God is Father, Son and Holy Spirit.' How might the story of Jesus' baptism in Mark be used to support belief about the Trinity? (4)

(d) (i) According to Mark, where did Jesus go immediately after his baptism? (2)
    (ii) 'What happened to Jesus immediately after his baptism is a great source of strength to Christians.' Explain this statement and say what you think about it. (4)

5. (a) When Jesus preached in his home town, Mark says that the people there rejected him.
    (i) What questions did they ask themselves about Jesus when they heard him preach? (4)
    (ii) What did Jesus say to them? (2)

(b) On another occasion, Jesus asked Peter what people were saying about him. Outline the conversation which followed. (4)

(c) What was the meaning of the term Peter used about Jesus? (4)

(d) 'Get away from me, Satan!' Why did Jesus say this to Peter? (2)

(e) 'People still ask themselves serious questions about who Jesus is. It is one of the most important things to think about.' What do you think about this statement? Give reasons for your views. (4)

6. Mark says that Jesus took Peter, James and John with him up a high mountain.

(a) Describe what happened on the mountain. (4)

(b) Explain the significance of Moses AND Elijah for Jews at the time of Jesus. (4)

(c) Mark says that Peter, James and John were badly frightened by what happened on the mountain.
    (i) Outline ONE other occasion when something Jesus does OR something which happens to him causes fear in others. (4)
    (ii) What do you think is the meaning of the fear experienced by Jesus' disciples? (4)

(d) 'To fear the Lord is the beginning of wisdom.' Do you think that for a religious person, fear can be a good thing? Give reasons for your views. (4)

7. (a) Mark tells how on one occasion, Jesus calmed a storm.
    (i) Describe what happened. (4)
    (ii) What possible lessons could Mark's first readers have drawn from this story? (4)

   (b) On another occasion Jesus cured a man who was possessed by a mob or legion of demons.
    (i) Outline the conversation Jesus had with this man while he was possessed. (4)
    (ii) How did the man's attitude towards Jesus change after his healing? (2)
    (iii) Name TWO other healing miracles recorded by Mark. (2)

   (c) 'Miracles do not happen today. Why should anybody believe in the miracles of Jesus?' How might a religious person respond to views like these? (4)

8. (a) Mark describes how Jesus healed a man with leprosy.
    (i) What did he say to Jesus? (2)
    (ii) How did Jesus respond? (2)
    (iii) What did Jesus forbid the man to do after he had been healed? (2)
    (iv) Explain why Jesus may have said this. (4)
    (v) What did Jesus tell him to do instead? (2)

   (b) Describe ONE occasion in Mark's Gospel in which Jesus heals a blind man. (4)

   (c) Jesus cared for the oppressed and the outcast. Describe TWO ways is which a religious person might try to follow his example today. (4)

9. (a) Mark describes how Jesus fed five thousand people.
    (i) What did Jesus use for this? (2)
    (ii) Describe what Jesus did with them. (4)
    (iii) Explain the possible hidden or symbolic meanings which might be present in this story. (4)

   (b) (i) Describe how Jesus healed Simon's mother-in-law. (4)
    (ii) What does Mark say she did after her illness left her? (2)

   (c) Mark records a large number of Jesus' miracles. Do you think that they present any problems for Christian belief today? (4)

10. (a) Mark tells miracle stories in order to demonstrate the power and authority of Jesus. Give TWO examples of Jesus healing somebody by a word of command. (2)

   (b) Jesus said to the paralysed man, 'Your sins are forgiven.'
    (i) What happened next? (4)
    (ii) Explain why the forgiveness of sins is such an important idea for Christians. (4)

   (c) Mark tells how Jesus healed a man with a paralysed hand on the Sabbath.
    (i) Why were some people annoyed by this? (4)
    (ii) What did they decide to do? (2)

   (d) 'Jesus shows us that it is not always right to avoid arguments.' What do you think about this idea? Give reasons for your views. (4)

11. (a) Mark often describes arguments between Jesus and the Pharisees.
    (i) Describe ONE such argument. (4)
    (ii) Explain the attitude of the Pharisees towards the Jewish Law. (4)
    (iii) How would you say Jesus' attitude towards the Jewish Law differed from that of the Pharisees? (4)

   (b) When Jesus was in Jerusalem, he was asked whether it was right to pay taxes to the Roman Emperor.
    (i) What did Jesus ask to see? (2)
    (ii) What did he say then? (2)

   (c) 'We must always obey the law.' Should a religious person agree with this statement? Give reasons for your views. (4)

12. (a) Describe the teaching of Jesus on marriage and divorce in Mark's Gospel. (4)

(b) Describe the usual view of divorce among Jews at the time of Jesus. (4)

(c) Mark describes how some members of the party of the Sadducees tried to trick Jesus with a question about rising from the dead.
   (i) Outline the story they told him. (4)
   (ii) Why was this an important issue for the Sadducees? (2)
   (iii) Give ONE other example of how the teaching of Jesus differed from that of the Jews of his time. (2)

(d) 'Jesus' teaching about marriage sets an unrealistic ideal.' What do you think about this statement? Give reasons for your views. (4)

13. (a) 'It is what comes out of a person that makes him unclean.' Explain how Jesus' attitude towards ritual cleanliness was different from that of other Jews of his time. (4)

(b) Describe ONE occasion which shows how Jesus' attitude towards sinners was different from the usual one of the people of his time. (4)

(c) Mark describes how Jesus spoke against the religious leaders of his time in the Parable of the Tenants in the Vineyard. Relate this parable. (4)

(d) When Jesus arrived at Jerusalem, Mark says that he visited the Temple. Describe what happened on this occasion. (4)

(e) 'When you look at the Gospel, you can understand why there has been so much bad feeling between Jews and Christians over the centuries.' Do you think this is a fair statement? What can be done to improve matters? (4)

14. Mark says that Jesus began his preaching immediately after John the Baptist had been put in prison.

(a) What was the message that Mark says Jesus proclaimed? (4)

(b) Describe the usual understanding of the Kingdom of God in the time of Jesus. (4)

(c) Mark records Jesus' parables.
   (i) What is a parable? (4)
   (ii) Why, according to Mark, did Jesus speak in parables? (4)

(d) 'Look at the world today! How could anybody say that the Kingdom of God has ever arrived?' What do you think about these views? Give reasons for your answer. (4)

15. (a) What is the difference between a parable and an allegory? (2)

(b) 'The Parable of the Tenants in the Vineyard is not really a parable at all. It is an allegory.' How would you support this claim? (4)

(c) (i) Relate the Parable of the Mustard Seed. (3)
   (ii) Give ONE possible conclusion Mark's first readers might have drawn from this parable. (2)
   (iii) Relate the Parable of the Seed Growing Secretly. (3)
   (iv) Give ONE idea about the Kingdom of God contained in this parable (2)

(d) 'It was not fair of Jesus to talk in parables. Why didn't he just say what he meant?' How would you respond to such a viewpoint? (4)

16. (a) According to Mark, the Parable of the Sower shows how different people respond to the news of the Kingdom. Explain how it depicts TWO types of person. (4)

(b) Explain why the Parable of the Sower might have been particularly encouraging for Mark's first readers. (4)

(c) Mark tells the story of how Jesus healed a man's son when the disciples had been unable to.
    (i)   Briefly describe the boy's symptoms. (2)
    (ii) Jesus said to the boy's father that everything was possible to those who had faith. What did the father say in reply? (2)
    (iii) Explain why Christians today might find the man's words encouraging. (4)

(d) 'Many people say they are Christians without thinking. Very few have real faith.' Do you agree or disagree? Give your reasons. (4)

17. (a) Mark describes how Jesus invited a rich man to sell everything he had, give the money to the poor, and follow him.
    (i)   What did the rich man do? (2)
    (ii) What did Jesus say when this happened? (2)
    (iii) How did Jesus' disciples react to Jesus' words? (2)

(b) On another occasion, Jesus was watching people as they gave money to the Temple treasury in Jerusalem.
    (i)   Who only gave a very small donation? (2)
    (ii) What did Jesus have to say about this? (4)

(c) Describe Jesus' attitude to wealth and money in Mark's Gospel. (4)

(d) 'Jesus' teaching makes very hard demands. Lots of people call themselves Christians, but very few really take his teachings seriously.' Do you think this is a fair statement? Give your reasons. (4)

18. (a) Mark describes how on one occasion Jesus found out that his disciples had been arguing about which one of them was the greatest.
    (i)   What did Jesus say? (2)
    (ii) What did he do then? (2)

(b) Give TWO possible reasons why Jesus taught that a child was the best model for his disciples. (4)

(c) On another occasion, James and John approached Jesus with a request.
    (i)   What did they ask for? (2)
    (ii) Jesus asked them a question in return. What was it? (2)
    (iii) Explain what Jesus said. (4)

(d) 'Jesus was rejected by his townsfolk, condemned by both Jews and Romans, and died abandoned and in disgrace. Many of his followers suffered cruelly. Why should anybody want to follow such a person?' What do you think? Give reasons for your views. (4)

19. (a) Jesus spoke about his own death to his disciples several times.
    (i)   Describe ONE occasion when he did this. (4)
    (ii) Explain why Jesus' disciples seem to have found his teaching about his forthcoming death so hard to take in. (4)

(b) Mark describes Jesus' anointing at the house of Simon the Leper in Bethany.
    (i)   Why did some people object to what the woman had done? (2)
    (ii) What did Jesus say about this? (2)
    (iii) How does Mark help his readers to understand the death of Jesus? (4)

(c) 'History is full of the deaths of innocent people. Why should the death of Jesus be considered so important?' What do you think about this point of view? Give your reasons. (4)

20. (a) The night before he died, Jesus ate a final meal with his disciples.
      (i)   Describe what he did with the bread during this meal.   (2)
      (ii) What did Jesus say when they drank from the cup?   (6)

    (b) Describe ONE modern Christian belief about the Eucharist.   (4)

    (c) 'Take this cup away from me!' Explain these words of Jesus.   (4)

    (d) Receiving Holy Communion on Sundays is neither here nor there. It's living a Christian life that counts.' What do you think about this statement? Give reasons for your views.   (4)

21. (a) 'My God, My God, why have you abandoned me?'
      (i)   When did Jesus say these words?   (2)
      (ii) Explain why you think he said them.   (4)
      (iii) Name ONE other person by whom Jesus had been recently abandoned. (2)

    (b) As he was dying, some people taunted Jesus. Relate one of the things they said, and explain it.   (4)

    (c) Describe fully what Joseph of Arimathea did after the death of Jesus.   (4)

    (d) 'The resurrection of Jesus makes no difference. His death was very, very sad.' What do you think about this statement? Give reasons for your views.   (4)

22. (a) Mark says that the Chief Priests and the teachers of the Law wanted to get rid of Jesus.
      (i)   Give TWO reasons why you think they might have wanted to do this. (2)
      (ii) What was their plan?   (4)

    (b) (i)   According to Mark, why did Pilate think that the religious authorities had handed Jesus over to him?   (2)
         (ii) How far do you think Pilate was responsible for Jesus' death?   (4)

    (c) The notice of Jesus' crime read 'The King of the Jews'. For what reasons do you think Mark recorded this information?   (4)

    (d) In what ways might the story of Jesus' crucifixion help Christians to face suffering?   (4)

23. (a) Mark's Gospel ends with some women visiting Jesus' tomb on the Sunday morning.
      (i)   What had they gone there to do?   (2)
      (ii) Explain why they had delayed their visit until Sunday.   (2)
      (iii) Describe what they saw.   (2)
      (iv) Relate the message they were given.   (4)
      (v) What was their reaction?   (2)

    (b) Explain why there are alternative endings to Mark's Gospel.   (4)

    (c) 'Jesus was raised from the dead. That is an historical fact, just like any other.' What do you think about this point of view? Give your reasons.   (4)

Index